Heaven Can't Wait

HEAVEN CAN'T WAIT

Living the _Really_ Good Life Now

ROBERT JEFFRESS

BROADMAN
& HOLMAN
PUBLISHERS

Nashville, Tennessee

Published by:
Broadman & Holman Publishers
Nashville, Tennessee

Printed in the United States of America

Design: Steven Boyd

4261-48
0-8054-6148-5

Dewey Decimal Classification: 248.4
Subject Heading: Christian Life \ Theology
Library of Congress Card Catalog Number: 94-8096

Library of Congress Cataloging-in-Publication Data

Jeffress, Robert, 1955–
Heaven can't wait : living the really good life now / by Robert Jeffress.
   p.   cm.
ISBN 0-8054-6148-5
1. Bible. N.T. Colossians III—Commentaries.   2. Jesus Christ—Kingdom.   I. Title.   II. Title: Heaven can't wait!
BS2715.3.J44   1995
248.4—dc20
                                              94-8096
                                              CIP

To my father, Robert James Jeffress, Sr.

—————

Truly, truly, I say to you,
he who hears My word, and believes Him who sent Me,
has eternal life, and does not come into judgment,
but has passed out of death into life.

— JOHN 5:24

Contents

✳

Introduction

When I began this book many months ago, our church was also commencing a massive renovation of our facilities. Over the years, our buildings had deteriorated and were in need of repair. Realizing that the project would take millions of dollars to complete, the renovation committee of our church chose to employ a financial consultant to help us raise the funds necessary to complete the project.

While the vast majority of our congregation enthusiastically supported the renovation project and the decision to employ a consultant, a few people had some legitimate questions. "How do you know it is God's will for us to enter such a massive project?" "Why do we need to do this *now?*" "Why do we need an organized fund-raising campaign? Shouldn't we just trust God to supply the needs?"

I began to see our renovation project as a metaphor for the Christian life. Because of the devastating effects of sin, all of our lives are in shambles. However, when we become a Christian, God begins a massive renovation of every area of our lives: our attitudes, our actions, and our affections. The foundation is laid when we become a Christian. But that initial decision to trust in Christ is not the end; it is the beginning of a lifelong building program: "As you therefore have received Christ Jesus the Lord, so walk in Him, having been firmly rooted and *now being built up* in Him and established in your faith" (Col. 2:6–7, emphasis mine).

How does God "renovate" our attitudes, actions, and affections? Some people would say it is through human effort alone. "Do your best to live by the Ten Commandments and the Golden Rule. That's all that God expects from you." Others would answer that the process of becoming like Jesus Christ is solely the work of God's Spirit. "You can't live the Christian life. God must live His life through you. Let go and let God," they counsel.

Admittedly, this all gets pretty confusing. What part does God play and what part do I play in living "the good life," i.e., becoming like Jesus Christ? As I have struggled with this dilemma in my life, I discovered a chapter in the Bible that clearly answers that question. Colossians 3 reminds us that we do not have to wait until heaven to enjoy "the good life." God's Spirit has given us both the desire and the power to transform our lives now. And Colossians 3 is the blueprint that will show us how.

✳

The Command
to Be Heavenly-Minded

If then you have been raised up with Christ, keep seeking the things above, where Christ is, seated at the right hand of God. Set your mind on the things above, not on the things that are on earth. For you have died and your life is hidden with Christ in God. When Christ, who is our life, is revealed, then you also will be revealed with Him in glory.

— Colossians 3:1–4

O N E

All This . . . and Heaven, Too?

"Show me your checkbook register, and I can immediately know your priorities in life."

Those words, coming from the radio of my Volkswagen Bug, struck me like a thunder bolt as I drove to church one Sunday morning, more than twenty years ago. As a high school student, I was working hard at a number of jobs and had accumulated an impressive amount of money. While I gave a tithe to my local church, I felt that the rest of my hard-earned money was mine to spend as I chose. It never occurred to me that how I spent the remaining 90 percent of my money reflected my true values in life.

That afternoon I went home and looked at my checkbook register. The majority of entries revealed the pursuits and interests of a typical high school boy:

➤ Gasoline
➤ McDonald's

➤ Gifts for my girlfriend (a good investment, since she became my wife!)

It dawned on me that, although I was declaring that spiritual pursuits were the most important aspect of my life, they were, in fact, receiving only my token financial support. I decided to rearrange my spending priorities. Within a few months, I had given away a large part of my assets to Christian ministries, and I began spending much of my current income to support evangelistic ministries at my high school. That Sunday afternoon spent reexamining my priorities and affections was a milestone in my spiritual life. I always think of it as my first "spiritual awakening."

Frankly, that adjustment in my spending priorities was relatively easy—especially compared to my second "spiritual awakening," which occurred several years ago. The catalyst for this awakening was again an honest, but painful, evaluation of my priorities and affections.

One morning, I read these words that jolted me out of my spiritual complacency:

> I believe that you can always determine a person's true character by what he seeks to gain and what he really loves. In fact, you could easily evaluate your own character by that same approach. Ask yourself this question: "What are the three things I am currently seeking most earnestly?" That will be a good monitor of whether your preoccupation is heavenly or earthly—Godward or selfward. If that doesn't work, ask yourself this: "What are the three things I love the most?" And if you can't figure out how to answer that question, ask yourself this one: "What are the three things I think about the most?"[1]

It's that last question that really got me: "What are the three things I think about the most?" My days, like your days, are filled with work, family, church, and social activities that demand my attention. There is not a lot of time for daydreaming and idle thoughts. Yet everyone has *some* time each day when his mind is free to wander. In those times, the writer was asking, where do your thoughts drift?

My free time to think occurs each morning while I am running. As I honestly evaluated what I found myself thinking about during those times, I was embarrassed. At the risk of forever ruining my reputation as a man of God, I will tell you what was occupying my thoughts during those free moments:

> ➤ Money
> ➤ Success (not success in building God's kingdom, but success in building mine)
> ➤ Potential vacation sites for the coming year
> ➤ Conflicts with people and how I could get the upper hand in them
> ➤ A few things not suitable for a Christian book!

How shocking! A man of the cloth not thinking about God all the time? Please don't misunderstand. I had a programmed "quiet time" every day for prayer, Bible reading, and journaling. But the area of my life that was being evaluated by the author's words was not activities, but affections. Very simply, the writer was saying that what I thought about in my free time was indicative of what I was pursuing and, consequently, what I loved most.

Jesus said virtually the same thing in Matthew 6:19–21: "Do not lay up for yourselves treasures upon earth, where moth and rust destroy, and where thieves break in and steal. But lay up for yourselves treasures in heaven, where neither moth nor rust destroys, and where thieves do not break in or steal; *for where your treasure is, there will your heart be also*" (emphasis mine).

Many Christians have a vague understanding of what Jesus was saying in these familiar words. But few can precisely explain what they mean—mainly because of a failure to understand what the word *heart* represented to the Jewish mind.

Whenever we think of the word *heart*, we think of the seat of emotions. People will often say, "I love you with all of my heart." Or, "I feel this in my heart." But in the Hebrew mind, the heart represented a person's *mind*. For example, Psalm 14:1 says, "The fool has said in his *heart*, 'There is no God,'" and Proverbs 23:7 says, "For as he thinketh in his *heart*, so is he" (KJV).

Why this short course on Hebrew anatomy? To understand what Jesus was saying in Matthew 6, we need to understand His and His disciples' concept of "heart." Jesus was talking about the mind. If He were speaking to a crowd today, He might say, "For where your treasure is, there will your *mind* be also."

As I honestly evaluated my affections, as revealed by my thoughts, I discovered that they were focused more on the temporal than on the eternal. I had preached enough sermons about eternal values to know that this was not a satisfactory situation. But how could I change?

I immediately realized that the job of transforming my affections, pursuits, and thoughts would be much more difficult than the change in my spending habits twenty years earlier. How does a person become heavenly-minded while still confined to the everyday responsibilities and temptations of life? This was my challenge.

God brought to mind a Scripture passage I had not looked at in a long time. It is found in the opening verses of Colossians 3: "If then you have been raised up with Christ, keep seeking the things above, where Christ is, seated at the right hand of God. Set your mind on the things above, not on the things that are on earth" (vv. 1-2).

As I continued to read, I discovered that Colossians 3 contained the answers I was seeking. In this chapter, Paul explained how we can live as citizens of heaven while still on earth. Paul reminded us that we need not and should not wait until heaven to become godly people in our thoughts, our affections, and our actions. For the next several weeks, I spent my morning running time memorizing and meditating on this chapter. Slowly, God began to reveal and explain through this chapter what it meant to be heavenly-minded.

I do not pretend to have "arrived." But I believe I have a much better understanding of how to "keep seeking the things above" while still a resident of this planet. This book is an attempt to share with you some of the things God has taught me in this process.

Take just a moment to ask yourself and answer the same questions that challenged me:

"What three things am I seeking most earnestly?"

1.
2.
3.

"What three things do I love the most?"

1.
2.
3.

"What are the three things I think about the most?"

1.
2.
3.

If your answers to the above questions were "love, joy, peace"; "God, Jesus, and the Holy Spirit"; and "obeying God, winning people to Christ, and how to squeeze more Bible study time into my schedule," you should not have bought this book. *You should have written it!*

But if you have experienced some of the same struggles I have mentioned in getting your affections and thoughts focused "on things above," I invite you to read on.

BETWEEN TWO WORLDS

Why is it so difficult for Christians to set their minds and affections on eternal things? Some might immediately answer, "Because of our sin nature." Certainly there is some truth in that. Christians do have two sets of desires that are warring against one another—the desires of the flesh and the desires of the Spirit.

Paul wrote of that conflict in Galatians 5:16–17: "But I say, walk by the Spirit, and you will not carry out the desire of the flesh. For the flesh sets its desire against the Spirit, and the Spirit against the flesh; for these are in opposition to one another, so that you may not do the things that you please."

But our difficulty in focusing on eternal values cannot be completely blamed on our sin nature. The fact is that God has placed Christians in a difficult (though not im-possible) situation. He asks Christians to be citizens of two worlds. In fact, so difficult is this predicament that it merited a special prayer by Jesus on our behalf:

> I have given them Thy word; and the world has hated them, because they are not of the world, even as I am not of the world. I do not ask Thee to take them out of the world, but to keep them from the evil one. They are not of the world, even as I am not of the world. Sanctify them in the truth; Thy word is truth. As Thou didst send Me into this world, I also have sent them into the world. (John 17:14–18)

Notice that twice in this passage Jesus declares that His followers are not of this world (vv. 14, 16). But twice Jesus specifically says that God's plan is not to take Christians out of this world, but to send them into the world (vv. 15, 18). And herein lies the tension. How can a Christian live in this world with its responsibilities and temptations without loving this world and being conformed to its values?

One finds this tension throughout the Bible. Look at some of the different Scripture passages that prohibit believers from loving and pursuing the values of this world:

For our citizenship is in heaven, from which also we eagerly wait for a Savior, the Lord Jesus Christ. (Phil. 3:20)

No soldier in active service entangles himself in the affairs of everyday life, so that he may please the one who enlisted him as a soldier. (2 Tim. 2:4)

Do not love the world, nor the things in the world. If anyone loves the world, the love of the Father is not in him. . . . And the world is passing away, and also its lusts; but the one who does the will of God abides forever. (1 John 2:15, 17)

Yet the Bible also speaks of some very definite responsibilities we have while here on earth. Think for just a moment about the areas of your life that are consuming your time and your thoughts. If you are like most Americans, you would probably answer:

➤ Work
➤ Family
➤ Money
➤ Health
➤ Friends
➤ Leisure

All of these qualify as earthly concerns, yet they are very much a part of our existence. And the Bible calls us to give attention and energy to each of these areas. For example:

1. Work: "Let him who steals steal no longer; but rather let him labor, performing with his own hands what is good, in order that he may have something to share with him who has need" (Eph. 4:28).

2. Family: "Husbands, love your wives, just as Christ also loved the church" (Eph. 5:25). "Train up a child in the way he should go, Even when he is old he will not depart from it" (Prov. 22:6).

3. Money: "Go to the ant, O sluggard, observe her ways and be wise, which, having no chief, officer, or ruler, prepares her food in the summer, and gathers her provision in the harvest. How long will you lie down, O sluggard? When will you arise from your sleep?" (Prov. 6:6–9).

4. Health: "Or do you not know that your body is a temple of the Holy Spirit who is in you, whom you have from God, and that you are not your own?" (1 Cor. 6:19).

5. Friends: "Two are better than one because they have a good return for their labor. For if either of them falls, the one will lift up his companion. But woe to the one who falls when there is not another to lift him up" (Eccl. 4:9–10).

6. Leisure: "Go then, eat your bread in happiness, and drink your wine with a cheerful heart; for God has already approved your works. . . . Enjoy life with the woman whom you love all the days of your fleeting life which He has given to you under the sun; for this is your reward in life, and in your toil in which you have labored under the sun" (Eccl. 9:7, 9).

So what is the answer? How can a Christian be heavenly-minded, while giving attention to God-given responsibilities here on earth? I believe the answer lies in properly defining the term *heavenly-minded.* What is Paul asking us to do when he admonishes us to set our "minds on the things above, not on the things that are on earth"?

He is not commanding us to rid ourselves of our vocational, social, financial, and family responsibilities. Nor is he suggesting that we view our earthly existence as an unwelcome hindrance to becoming godly people.

Instead, Paul is saying that being heavenly-minded is not as much a question of activities as it is of attitudes, affections, and adherence to God's commands. For example, would anyone really label a televangelist who wins thousands of people to Christ, but does so out of greed, as being heavenly-minded? And does it make sense to label a plumber who spends eight hours a day unclogging drains, yet loves the Lord with all of his heart, as someone who is "earthly-minded"? My point is obvious.

What then does it mean to be heavenly-minded? Based on Colossians 3, I think this definition is appropriate:

> *To be heavenly-minded means to conform our everyday affections, attitudes, and <u>actions</u> to the image of Christ.*

Being heavenly-minded simply means loving what Jesus loves, thinking like Jesus thinks, and behaving in every situation as Jesus would behave. Colossians 3 will show us how to do that. Chapter 3 falls into four major sections that can be outlined as followed:

The Command to Be Heavenly-Minded, Colossians 3:1–4. Paul explains why a Christian is to be focused on the eternal, rather than the temporal.

The Results of Being Heavenly-Minded, Colossians 3:5–14. Paul draws the relationship between heavenly thoughts and earthly actions.

The Steps to Becoming Heavenly-Minded, Colossians 3:15–17. Paul gives four steps to help Christians think, and therefore act, like kingdom citizens now.

The Evidence of Being Heavenly-Minded, Colossians 3:18–4:1. In these final verses, Paul details the two specific tests to determine if we have truly developed a heavenly mind-set.

The Joy of Living in Two Worlds

This first chapter has centered on the tension of being in the world and yet not of the world. Such a task is not easy. But there is a corresponding joy that overshadows the difficulties. There is something liberating about realizing that, "This world is not my home. I'm just a passing through."[2]

I will never forget the night I was called as pastor of the First Baptist Church in Eastland, Texas. It was one of the happiest and most satisfying experiences of my life. For the previous seven years, I had served as an associate pastor in a large church in Dallas. While I had enjoyed my work, I had always dreamed of being a pastor. This particular summer evening represented the realization of those dreams. After the church voted and we announced our decision to accept the church's call, my wife and I immediately placed our membership in our new church. We spent hours in a receiving line hugging, laughing, and crying with our new members. When we returned to the motel that evening, we were so excited we could barely sleep.

However, I still had responsibilities to fulfill at my former church. So, the next morning we drove back to Dallas, ready to finish our work there. The following six weeks was one of the strangest periods of my life. I was living in two worlds. My work was at the church in Dallas, but my membership and future was at the church in Eastland.

I honestly enjoyed those last six weeks of work in Dallas more than I had the previous seven years of my ministry there. Why? The fact that I would soon be leaving removed all the stress from my job. I could do what I felt was right, say what I thought was true, without any fear of the consequences. After all, I was leaving. What could they do to me?

But strangely, the fact that I would soon be leaving also gave me a fresh desire for excellence in my work as a minister. There was something about being called by the Eastland church as pastor that made me realize the seriousness of my vocation. So I also experienced a renewed zeal in my work that began those final weeks in Dallas and carried over into my ministry in Eastland.

Living as citizens of heaven while still residents of earth should give all of us the same liberation and motivation—liberation from the stress of this life, since our time here is so limited, and motivation to develop the attitudes and character that we will carry into eternity.

✳

ACTION STEPS

1. If someone were to examine your checkbook, what could they tell about your real interests in life? _____

_____

_____

_____

2. What did your answers to the questions on page 9 reveal to you about your pursuits, affections, and thoughts? Do you qualify as a heavenly-minded Christian?

_____

_____

_____

_____

3. According to the author, what is a heavenly-minded Christian? _____

_____

_____

_____

4. Recall a period in your life when you had truly "set your mind on the things above." Describe what your life was like during that time. _____

_____

_____

_____

5. What spiritual need(s) in your life prompted you to purchase this book? What are you hoping to change in your life as a result of this study? _____

_____

_____

_____

6. Memorize Colossians 3:1–2.

T W O

Wanted: Dead and *Alive!*

Max Lucado retells an interesting incident in the life of the great military leader Napoleon. One day the commander's prized steed ran away from him. An alert private immediately jumped on a horse and chased after the steed. When the private returned the horse to the general, Napoleon smiled at the private and said, "Thank you, *Captain!*"

The overjoyed private immediately took his old uniform to the quartermaster and exchanged it for that of a captain. He then ran back to the barracks, packed his bags, and moved into the officers' quarters. In an instant, the commander-in-chief had changed his status from that of a lowly private to that of a commissioned officer. He never once doubted the commander's words. Instead, he believed what the general had said and acted accordingly.[1]

In the same way, Jesus Christ has by a single act forever changed our status before God. By His death and resurrection, He has transformed believers from *enemies* of God to *children* of God. And now our responsibility is to act in a way that is consistent with our new status.

That is what Colossians 3 is all about. In this chapter, Paul urged us to exchange the old affections, attitudes, and actions that were characteristic of our former lives for those that are in concert with our new rank. Such a change is the essence of being "heavenly-minded." In the first chapter we used this definition that will guide our study of Colossians 3:

> *To be heavenly-minded means to conform our everyday affections, attitudes, and <u>actions</u> to the image of Christ.*

Is such a transformation possible now, or must we wait until heaven to become like Christ? The apostle Paul insists that such a change *is* possible *now*, in light of the death, resurrection, and glorification of Jesus Christ.

Affections + Thoughts = Actions

Let's look in more detail at Paul's command found in Colossians 3:1–2: "If then you have been raised up with Christ, keep seeking the things above, where Christ is, seated at the right hand of God. Set your mind on the things above, not on the things that are on earth."

Notice that there are two commands here: "keep seeking the things above" and "set your mind on the things above." Some people see these commands as one in the same, but they really aren't. The *New International Version* correctly distinguishes the two commands: "set your *hearts* on things above . . . set your *minds* on things above."

The order here is crucial. Paul was saying that we must first set our affections on the things above. Out of that readjustment of our affections, there should come a transformation in our thoughts and, ultimately, our actions.

Paul said the path to true and lasting change begins with a change of desires that leads to a change of thoughts and results in a change of actions.

Fine, Paul. But what are we to think about and desire? Twice Paul mentioned "the things above" (vv. 1–2). Now it does not take a rocket scientist to figure out that if you are going to be heavenly-minded, you need to love and think about things above. But what are "the things above"?

To artists in the Middle Ages, "the things above" were ornate physical objects that they were certain would be found in the heavens. Martin Luther lambasted those artists for their corrupt perceptions: "Oh, that heaven of the charlatans, with its golden chair and Christ seated at the Father's side vested in a choir cope and a golden robe, as the painters love to portray Him!"[2]

Today heaven means different things to different people. My three-year-old daughter is looking forward to heaven because she is convinced that there is an unlimited supply of toys there. Some older members in my congregation are anticipating heaven because it represents an end of their physical suffering. For me, heaven means seeing my parents again. Yes, heaven does hold the promise of all kinds of future pleasures. But is that really what Paul meant by "the things above"? Is being heavenly-minded simply a case of looking forward to the untold joys that await us in eternity?

Paul clarified what he meant by "the things above" with this phrase: "where Christ is, seated at the right hand of God." This concept of Jesus being seated at the right hand of God the Father is indicative of His power and position (see Ps. 110:1). Thus, Paul was not asking us to love and meditate on the *things* in heaven (which would involve a great deal of speculation), but on the qualities that characterize the life and rule of Jesus Christ who is in heaven.

Throughout the Bible we find lists of "the things above" which we are to seek:

But the fruit of the Spirit is love, joy, peace, patience, kindness, goodness, faithfulness, gentleness, self-control; against such things there is no law. (Gal. 5:22–23)

Finally, brethren, whatever is true, whatever is honorable, whatever is right, whatever is pure, whatever is lovely, whatever is of good repute, if there is any excellence and if anything worthy of praise, let your mind dwell on these things. (Phil. 4:8)

But the wisdom from above is first pure, then peaceable, gentle, reasonable, full of mercy and good fruits, unwavering, without hypocrisy. (Jas. 3:17)

And so we have come full circle back to our original definition of what it means to be heavenly-minded. Being heavenly-minded means to continually pursue those qualities that characterize the life of Jesus Christ. As we seek those qualities and think about them, they will transform our lives.

But is it really possible to conform our affections, thoughts, and actions to the image of Christ while we are here on earth? In these opening verses of Colossians 3, Paul assured us that such a transformation *is* possible when we understand our relationship to the death, resurrection, and glorification of Jesus Christ.

True Possibility Thinking

Maybe you have heard the story about the farmer who had spent his entire life in the backwoods of West Virginia. He married his childhood sweetheart and they raised their five children without once leaving their home turf. One day, the father began to realize that if his kids were ever going to amount to anything more than he had been, he would need to broaden their horizons. So he and Mama began to save their money for an excursion to the big city. After several years, they finally had the money necessary for the adventure. They decided that they would stay in the fanciest hotel in the city and enjoy all of the sights of the metropolis.

The day for the big trip finally arrived. They loaded up their truck, and off they went. As they pulled up to the front of the hotel, the father said, "Mama, you and the children stay in the truck, while Junior and I go in to check the place out."

So the father and his oldest son ventured inside the lobby. They were dumbfounded by what they saw. Hanging from the vaulted ceiling shone a huge, glittering chandelier—something they had never seen before. In the middle of the lobby was an indoor waterfall. The perimeter of the lobby was filled with multitudes of dazzling boutiques.

But what really caught their attention was a clicking sound they kept hearing behind them. When they turned around, they saw a small room that people were walking into. People would press a button, lights would flicker above the door, then "click," the door would open. Some people would walk out, while others walked in. Then the doors would shut again.

After a few minutes, Dad noticed a little, old, wrinkled lady who walked up to the door and pressed the button. Soon the door opened, she walked in, and the door closed. In less than a minute, the door opened again, and out walked a beautiful, blond woman in her early twenties. As she walked by, she winked at Dad and Junior. They were speechless. Finally, in slow, deliberate words, Dad nudged his son and said, "Junior, go git Mama!"[3]

All of us are enthralled at the possibility of transformation. The resurrection of Jesus Christ reminds us that real and lasting change is possible. And it's possible *now!* I believe that is why Paul began his discussion of being heavenly-minded by alluding to the greatest victory of all time: the resurrection of Jesus Christ.

The opening clause in Colossians 3:1 could be translated, "*Since* you have been raised up with Christ, keep seeking the things above." Paul assumed that his readers were believers and therefore had already participated in the resurrection life of Christ.

"Wait a minute! Already participated? I thought the resurrection was still future." Yes and no. There is a resurrection of our physical bodies that is still in the future (see 1 Thess. 4). But Christ has already been raised from the dead. And if you are in Christ, you should be sharing in that resurrected life right now.

What does it mean to share in Christ's resurrected life? In Romans 6:4 Paul described it as a new *quality* of life: "Therefore we have been buried with Him through baptism into death, in order that as Christ was raised from the dead through the glory of the Father, so we too might walk *in newness of life*" (emphasis mine). Paul was saying that the attitudes and actions that characterized the life of Christ can and should be ours because we have been raised up with Christ.

Stop for just a moment and ask yourself, "What do I admire most about the life of Jesus Christ?"

His love for others?

His singular devotion to obeying God?

His peace in the midst of trials?

His boldness in confronting sin?

His power?

All of those things can belong to you *now* if you are a Christian. The same power that raised Christ from the dead is available in your life *now*.

REST IN PEACE

Paul gave a second reason that we can transform our affections, attitudes, and actions to the image of Jesus Christ. Not only have we participated in His resurrection, we have also participated in His death: "For you have died and your life is hidden with Christ in God" (Col. 3:3).

You may be checking your pulse and saying, "As far as I can tell, I'm still alive. What do you mean I have died?" The Bible says that when you trusted in Christ, in some inexplicable way, God propelled you back two thousand years ago to the cross and nailed your old nature—those desires contrary to the character of Christ—to the cross. The absolute power that sin held over your life was destroyed.

Of course, the natural question is, "If my sin nature has been destroyed, why do I still sin?" If you have ever had the unfortunate experience of seeing a chicken with its head cut off, you can understand this concept. Even though the chicken has been dealt a death blow, it continues to flop around the barnyard for awhile. In the same way, Jesus Christ delivered a death blow to your sinful nature when He died on the cross. Yes, there will still be some residual effects of that old nature in your life. But sin will have no more power over your life than you choose to allow.

In summary, Paul was saying that when we become Christians, the power of our old nature—those affections, attitudes, and actions that are opposed to the will of God—has been destroyed. Therefore, we should live in a way that validates the fact that sin's power has been destroyed. Again, look at Paul's words in Romans 6: "knowing this, that our old self was crucified with Him, that our body of sin might be done away with, that we should no longer be slaves to sin; for he who has died is freed from sin. . . . Even so consider yourselves to be dead to sin, but alive to God in Christ Jesus" (Rom. 6:6–7, 11).

Dr. J. Vernon McGee used to tell the story of a woman who lived in the Deep South and had been married for a number of years to her childhood sweetheart. Although their marriage was not perfect, it was still enjoyable. Suddenly, the husband died of a heart attack. The wife was so overtaken with grief that she could not bear to part with him. So she had him embalmed and placed him in a chair, sealed up in a glass case that was placed just inside the front door of their large plantation home.

Each time she walked into the front door, she would smile and say, "Hi, John, how are you?" Then she would go on about her business. This continued day after day, month after month.

About a year later, she decided to take a trip to Europe. While there, she met a man who swept her off her feet. They were so enthralled with one another that they married within a few weeks and honeymooned throughout the continent. Finally, it was time to return to the States. They had decided they would live in her home.

As the groom carried his bride over the threshold of their new home, he almost dropped her on the floor when he saw Old John sitting in his chair in the glass case.

"Who is this?"

"Well, that is John. He was my husband . . . "

"He is history; he's dead!"

The new husband carried John to the backyard, dug a hole, and buried him![4]

In the same way, many Christians make the mistake of forgetting that their old nature is dead and powerless. Instead, they build a shrine for it and acknowledge it every day of their lives as though it were still alive. Paul is reminding us that our old nature is dead; therefore, we should bury it once for all!

EXCHANGING THE PLEASURE FOR THE TREASURE

Paul gave a final motivation for us to become heavenly-minded now: the future glorification of Jesus Christ. Any temporary suffering or loss we accrue in this life for saying no to our old nature and its desires will be more than compensated for in heaven: "Your life is hidden with Christ in God. When Christ, who is our life, is revealed, then you also will be revealed with Him in glory" (Col. 3:3).

I think we make a tremendous mistake when we under-estimate how difficult it is to shift our affections and pursuits from the earthly to the eternal. The great comedian Jack Benny, known for his miserly ways and his love for money, had a famous routine in which he was held up by an armed robber.

"Your money or your life!" the thief demanded.

No reply from Benny.

"I said, 'Your money or your life!'"

Again, no reply.

Impatiently, the thief cried, "Well . . . ?"

Benny answered, "Don't rush me! I'm still thinking!"[5]

Pursuing "the things above" rather than "the things on earth" does require a choice. As we will see in the next two chapters, it involves saying no to some very natural and satisfying activities. Why give up those things?

When I was a youth, I used to hear preachers say that even if heaven turned out to be a myth, they would still have no regrets about being a Christian. They proclaimed that the Christian life was the most satisfying life available. Sin held no real pleasure.

Baloney. Paul says that "if we have hoped in Christ in this life only, we are of all men most to be pitied" (1 Cor. 15:19). Why? Because we have given up some very satisfying pursuits for something that does not exist. Make no mistake about it, "the things that are on earth" are quite pleasurable. The *only* reason to give them up is if something better awaits us.

Hebrews 11 lists several men and women who chose the eternal over the temporal because they believed something better awaited them. I love the passage describing Moses' choice: "By faith Moses, when he had grown up, refused to be called the son of Pharaoh's daughter; choosing rather to endure ill-treatment with the people of God, than to enjoy the passing pleasures of sin; considering the reproach of Christ greater riches than the treasures of Egypt; for he was looking to the reward" (Heb. 11:24–26).

Notice what Moses gave up. The writer of Hebrews did not say "the emptiness of sin" and "the filthy lucre of Egypt." No, he described it in appealing terms: "the passing *pleasures* of sin" and "the *treasures* of Egypt." Why would Moses give up those things? One reason: He was looking forward to a future reward that would far outweigh temporary pleasure and riches.

Paul alluded to this same reward. There is a time coming when Christ, who is now hidden from the world, will be unveiled to the world. At that time, every knee will bow and every tongue will confess that Jesus Christ is Lord (see Col. 3:4 and Phil. 2:10–11). And at that time every Christian will be vindicated.

Today, the person who pursues "the things above" is often misunderstood, ridiculed, even persecuted. But some day that will all change. When the unbelieving world sees the glory of Christ revealed, they will understand why His followers were willing to sacrifice the temporal pleasures of this world.

The ancient Romans were noted for their enduring achievements in construction. If you visit Rome today, you will see many of the Roman arches still standing after two thousand years. What was their secret? The Romans had an interesting policy. When they finished building an arch, the engineer in charge of the project was asked to stand beneath the arch when the scaffolding was removed. If the arch did not hold, he was the first to know it!

In the same way, when Christ returns, the entire world will see that those who have set their hearts and minds on things above did indeed build their lives correctly.

✳

Action Steps

1. Explain "the things above." _____
_____
_____
_____

2. If you could change anything about your Christian life, what would it be? Do you believe change is possible?
_____
_____
_____

3. If you are a Christian, in what sense have you been "raised up with Christ"? _____
_____
_____
_____

4. Identify the areas in your life in which you are most tempted to sin. What does Colossians 3:3 say to you about the power of sin in your life? _____
_____
_____
_____

5. What pleasures or pursuits are you voluntarily forfeiting in order to pursue "the things above"? _____
_____
_____
_____

6. If you were to stand before the judgment seat of Christ today, how do you think Jesus Christ would evaluate your life? _____
_____
_____

7. Memorize Colossians 3:3–4.

The Results of Being Heavenly-Minded

And so, as those who have been chosen of God, holy and beloved, put on a heart of compassion, kindness, humility, gentleness and patience; bearing with one another, and forgiving each other, whoever has a complaint against anyone; just as the Lord forgave you, so also should you. And beyond all these things put on love, which is the perfect bond of unity.

— Colossians 3:12–14

Just Say No!

I recently read a newspaper article detailing scandals among well-known entertainers and political figures. One of the sections of the article dealt with a prominent actor who was arrested a few years ago for having made a pornographic videotape in a hotel room with several women. The writer said that in a "strange twist of irony" the actor had appeared in a movie before this incident playing a character caught in exactly the same situation— making pornographic videos. What the writer labeled "strange" and "coincidental" was very understandable to me.

This actor had obviously spent hours studying his character, memorizing his lines, and then filming the scenes. As the actor meditated on this character's immoral activities, those activities began to take root in his thoughts. The more the actor thought about what the character had done, the more his own lusts were aroused. His final act, which brought about his downfall, was simply the natural result of his thoughts.

The apostle Paul made the same connection between thoughts and behavior in Colossians 3. What we love and what we think about determine how we behave. That is why Paul urged us to set our hearts and minds "on the things above, not on the things that are on earth."

CHANGING YOUR BEHAVIOR

Let's take a moment and review what Paul has already said. First, he called us to be heavenly-minded Christians. Being heavenly-minded does not mean shirking our present responsibilities in life and moving to a monastery. Instead, a heavenly-minded Christian is one who is in the process of conforming her or his affections, attitudes, and actions to the image of Christ. Being heavenly-minded means loving what Jesus loves, thinking as Jesus thinks, and behaving as Jesus would behave in every circumstance.

Second, Paul assured us that such a radical transformation of our affections, attitudes, and actions is possible in light of our participation in the resurrection, death, and glorification of Jesus Christ. The same mighty power that lifted Jesus out of the grave is available to transform our lives when we become Christians. In addition to that, our old affections, attitudes, and actions that were opposed to God have been put to death. They have no power over us.

Finally, Paul reminded us that we will someday share in the same glory and honor that will come to the Lord Jesus Christ when He is revealed to the world. Any loss we have experienced in this life for our obedience to Christ will be amply rewarded in the next life. Such a realization should be a motivation for us to seek the things above.

Paul has now drawn the relationship between loving and thinking about the things above with our every-day actions. If indeed our chief pursuit in life is becoming like Jesus Christ, there should be some corresponding changes in our behavior.

You Only Die Twice?

Beginning in verse 5, Paul resumed his thought about the death of our old nature. But this time Paul was more interested in the practical implications rather than the theological explanation of this profound truth. "Therefore consider the members of your earthly body as dead to immorality, impurity, passion, evil desire, and greed, which amounts to idolatry."

Paul has already explained that our old nature has been crucified. But how does that truth apply to our behavior now? Some translations of Colossians 3:5 seem to indicate that we must *again* crucify our old nature: "Put to death, therefore, whatever belongs to your earthly nature" (NIV); "Mortify therefore your members which are upon the earth" (KJV); "Put to death therefore what is earthly in you" (RSV).

Why would a second execution of our old nature be necessary? Was Christ's work on the cross incomplete? Must we be expected to finish what He began? Certainly such an idea would be contrary to Paul's major theme in Colossians—the sufficiency of Jesus Christ.

I think that the *New American Standard Version* best captures Paul's thoughts: "Therefore *consider* the members of your earthly body as dead" (emphasis mine). We are to act in a way that is consistent with the theological truth of our old nature's death.

"Robert, aren't you asking me to play a game here? Are you saying that I am to pretend sin has no appeal to me and no power over me?" I will admit that is what it sounds like. I used to be bothered as a teenager by Bible teachers who would tell me my sin nature was dead and powerless. Yet my everyday experience was not consistent with that truth. I could identify with the teenager who said, "I got saved six months ago, but nobody told my hormones!"

Paul did not ask us to play any games here. He *did* ask us to connect spiritual reality with our everyday experience. For example, I am a thirty-eight-year-old man. For me to put on a skirt, high heels, and lipstick would be totally inconsistent with who I am—it would make no sense. In the same way, Paul says we ought to act in a way that is consistent with what has already happened to us spiritually.

My friend Bobb Biehl, president of Masterplanning International, tells an interesting story about a day he spent working in a circus and an important truth he learned:

> When we got there, it was a hot, dusty, windy day at the fairgrounds where the circus was playing. We moved props from one of the three rings to the next, helped in any way we could, and generally got dusty, dirty, tired and hungry.
>
> During one of the breaks, I started chatting with the man who trains the animals for Hollywood movies. "How is it that you can stake down a ten-ton elephant with the same size stake that you use for this little fellow?" I asked. (The "little fellow" weighed about three hundred pounds.)
>
> "It's easy when you know two things: elephants really do have great memories, but they really aren't very smart. When they are babies, we stake them down. They try to tug away from the stake maybe ten-thousand times before they realize that they can't possibly get away. At that point, their 'elephant memory' takes over and they remember for the rest of their lives that they can't get away from the stake."[1]

Paul was saying that sin has no more control over a Christian than a small stake has over a twenty-thousand pound elephant! Christ has freed us from the power of sin. Therefore, we are to behave in a way consistent with that truth. The word that is translated "mortify" in the *King James Version* and "consider . . . as dead" in the *New American Standard Version* means simply to *deal decisively with sinful actions and attitudes in our life.* Later in this chapter we will look at some specific ways to "deal decisively" with these sins, but first, let's see what sins Paul had in mind. You will notice in this catalog of sin that Paul moved from the specific to the general. He began with the overt action—immorality—and then traced the origin of such sin.

Immorality

First, Paul said that we are to consider our bodies as "dead" or free from the power of immorality. The word translated "immorality" is the Greek word *porneia*, from which we get our word *pornography.* The word denotes any sexual activity outside of the bonds of marriage: adultery, premarital sex, homosexuality, incest, prostitution, or bestiality. Examine Paul's writings and you will find that he frequently mentioned this sin first (see 1 Cor. 6:9–10; Gal. 5:14–21; Eph. 5:3–5).

One of the older members of my congregation asked me recently, "Pastor, why do you talk so much about sex in your messages?" The question caused me to momentarily wonder if I was unbalanced in my preaching. Or, maybe I was allowing my own struggles and temptations to inordinately color my sermons. But then it dawned on me that the reason I mentioned sex so often was that the Bible speaks about it so often, as the above passages confirm.

Was Paul hung up about sex? Why did he refer to it so frequently? I think two reasons may explain the apostle's emphasis on this subject. First of all, the call for sex only within the marriage relationship was a revolutionary concept in Paul's culture. The pagan religions not only permitted sex outside of marriage, they prescribed it as part of their religious rituals. But Christians were called to a radical lifestyle that would set them apart from any other religions. For a Christian to fall back into immorality was inconsistent with his claim of a new life. In Colossians 3:7, Paul reminded his readers that immorality was a part of their *old* lifestyle: "and in them you also once walked, when you were living in them."

By the way, the idea of sex only within the marriage relationship is just as radical today as it was in Paul's day. In a day when sexually transmitted diseases are killing tens of thousands of people each year, you would think that people might be more inclined to follow God's prescription for sex—one man with one woman for life. But just mention the idea of abstinence before marriage or fidelity to one's spouse, and people will think you stepped off of another planet.

Paul had a second reason for consistently condemning immorality—a reason that is directly tied to the theme of becoming heavenly-minded. In Paul's estimation, no sin jeopardized the process of sanctification (the theological term for the transformation of our affections, attitudes, and actions to the image of Christ) more than sexual sin.

All sin is displeasing to God, but immorality completely disrupts the process of our becoming heavenly-minded. That is why Paul wrote, "For this is the will of God, your sanctification; that is, that you abstain from sexual immorality; that each of you know how to possess his own vessel in sanctification and honor, not in lustful passion, like the Gentiles who do not know God" (1 Thess. 4:3).

Notice the link between sanctification and sexual purity. Why does immorality destroy the process of sanctification in a Christian's life? There does not seem to be a logical answer to that question. To many people, sex is a physiological function like eating and drinking. No big deal. Yet there is something about sexual sin that reaches into the innermost being of a person and holds him or her hostage.

I think about a well-known pastor who was caught in an immoral relationship with another woman. He had a loving family, a growing ministry, and plenty of money. Yet he was unwilling to give up his immoral lifestyle. When confronted about his sin, he said, "For years I have been doing what everyone else wanted me to do. Now I am going to do what I want to do." Why would a person give up his family, his ministry, and his financial security for a mere physiological function?

Sex is more than physiology. When a person is involved in sexual immorality, he is not just simply joining his body to another person, he joins his entire being to that person.

Impurity

Next, Paul mentions that we need to deal decisively with impurity in our lives. Immorality is not an isolated activity. When the above-mentioned pastor's sexual sin became public, people were shocked. "How could such a man of God suddenly fall into sin?" A person does not suddenly fall into adultery, or premarital sex, or homosexuality. Instead, there is a logical progression. Before the final plunge into immorality, there is impurity.

The word *impurity* literally means "uncleanness" and was used in the Old Testament to denote those people or objects that were ceremonially unclean. In the New Testament the word refers to moral uncleanness. It refers to a person whose mind, thoughts, and speech are saturated with moral filthiness.

You probably know such a person. His speech is filled with obscenities or dirty jokes. His conversation is rarely without sexual innuendo. Paul says such behavior is just one step away from the overt act of immorality. Impurity has no place in the life of one who seeks things above: "But do not let immorality or any impurity or greed even be named among you, as is proper among saints; and there must be no filthiness and silly talk, or coarse jesting, which are not fitting, but rather giving of thanks" (Eph. 5:3–4).

Passion and Evil Desires

"Therefore consider the members of our earthly body as dead to immorality, impurity, *passion, evil desire*" (emphasis mine). These words seem to belong together. "Passion and evil desire" refer to God-given desires that are misdirected. One of the greatest misconceptions in the world is that the Bible treats sex as sinful. The fact is that God created sex. It was all His idea! Moses reminded us that "For this cause a man shall leave his father and his mother, and shall cleave to his wife; and they shall become one flesh" (Gen. 2:24).

Sex is not sinful. Sin occurs when we try to fulfill our God-given sexual desires outside of God's will. And such sin never begins in the bedroom but in the heart. Remember Jesus' words in Matthew 5:27–28: "You have heard that it was said, 'You shall not commit adultery'; but I say to you, that everyone who looks on a woman to lust for her has committed adultery with her already in his heart."

What do Jesus and Paul mean by lust? They are not condemning simply admiring someone else's beauty. Instead, they are referring to a full-scale fantasy that involves a mental undressing and seduction with someone other than our spouse. Such fantasies lead to impurity that often results in overt immorality.

Greed

The final sin that Paul urged us to deal with is "greed, which amounts to idolatry." At first glance, this term seems out of place in the list. The first four terms all deal with sexual misbehavior. Why did Paul then mention greed? Remember, Paul was explaining the progression that leads to immorality. And so he was saying that at the root of immorality is greed (or in some versions, "covetousness").

Covetousness is simply an obsession with having more. It might be an intense desire for more money, or a better position, or a bigger home, or a finer car, or someone else's spouse. Although we think of greed as only having to do with money, it is in fact the root cause of many sins. I believe that is why we find the prohibition against covetousness as the climax of the Ten Commandments: "You shall not covet your neighbor's house; you shall not covet your neighbor's wife or his male servant or his female servant or his ox or his donkey or anything that belongs to your neighbor" (Ex. 20:17). Look at all of the other sins condemned in the Ten Commandments—theft, adultery, murder, idolatry—and at the root of most of these sins is an obsession with having more.

We see that truth illustrated throughout the Bible. Lucifer was cast down from heaven because of his desire for more. Eve ate the forbidden fruit because she wanted more. Lot's desire for a better land caused him to settle in Sodom. Jacob's desire for more inheritance caused him to cheat his brother Esau. Joseph's brothers' desire for more attention from their father caused them to sell Joseph into slavery. David's desire for more caused him to fall into adultery with Bathsheba. Solomon's desire for more wealth, power, and pleasure caused him to turn away from God.

Notice that Paul equates greed with idolatry: "greed which amounts to idolatry." Greed stems from the false belief that anyone or anything other than God can satisfy our deepest needs. The same error that causes a native in Africa to bow before a wooden idol causes many in our culture to bow down before the false idols of money, power, and sensual pleasure.

Greed is at the heart of all sensual behavior. As one writer observed: "This is why many middle-aged men who were once devoted to sensuality are now equally given to money. These sins have the same source."[2] Such idolatry is the antithesis of being heavenly-minded.

Dealing Decisively with the Sensual

We have spent some time explaining the meaning and progression of immoral behavior. But such an understanding is not enough to eradicate such behavior from our lives. Remember Paul's words in 3:5? We must put these actions and attitudes to death. Just has Christ delivered the death blow to the *power* of sin, we must daily destroy the *influence* of sin in our lives.

Let me suggest four practical steps that will help you "put to death" those sensual attitudes and actions that are a part of your old nature:

1. *Refuse to allow immoral thoughts to take residence in your mind.* Have you ever had the experience of hearing someone knock at your front door at 3:00 a.m.? If so, you know what an unnerving experience it is. You stumble out of bed, turn on the porch light, look through the peep hole in the door. If they are not recognizable, no matter how insistent they are, you don't open the door.

We need to protect our minds as we protect our homes. Just as we cannot control who knocks on our front door, we cannot always control the thoughts that seek residence in our minds. But we can determine if such thoughts are heavenly or earthly, and deal with them accordingly. I believe that is what Paul meant by "taking every thought captive to the obedience of Christ" (2 Cor. 10:5).

2. *Amputate sensual activity in your life.* What if immorality, impurity, or lust already has a grip on your life? What should you do? Again, note Paul's strong words. You are to put those activities and attitudes to death. The idea of putting something to death carries the image of destruction and violence. It is the same image Jesus used in Matthew 5:28–30:

> But I say to you, that everyone who looks on a woman to lust for her has committed adultery with her already in his heart. And if your right eye makes you stumble, tear it out, and throw it from you; for it is better for you that one of the parts of your body perish, than for your whole body to be thrown into hell. And if your right hand makes you stumble, cut it off, and throw it from you; for it is better for you that one of the parts of your body perish, than for your whole body to go into hell.

The idea of losing an eye or hand is painful. But remember, in Jesus' day there were no anesthetics to lessen the pain, only crude cutting tools. Imagine the trauma of having a doctor saw off a limb or cut out an eye. Yet Jesus said it would be better to endure such a horrific experience than to suffer the eternal consequences of sin.

Some have tried to dismiss this passage by saying that Jesus should not be taken literally here. They point out that even if you remove one eye, or one hand, there is still another to sin. True. But don't miss His point. We need to deal decisively with sin before it spreads. And sometimes that can be painful.

Suppose your arm was mangled in an accident. The blood supply is cut off, and gangrene sets in. What do you suppose a doctor would say? He would say that the arm has to come off. It might be painful and inconvenient. But without the operation, the whole body could be infected. In the same way, if your life has already been infected with immorality, radical surgery is essential!

Let me be very specific at this point. Are there magazines you read, television programs or movies you view that are making it difficult for you to be heavenly-minded? If so, cut them out of your life! Is your job a source of temptation where you cannot gain victory? If so, cut it out of your life—even if it means a change in jobs or less money. Are you involved in an immoral relationship? If so, cut it out of your life!

In one of my former churches, a man named Jerry came to visit me about a personal problem. Jerry was involved in a friendship with Darla who worked in his office. Darla was going through a painful divorce and was desperately in need of friendship. Jerry started spending his lunch hours counseling with Darla. After work they would sometimes meet for a short visit and snack before going to their respective homes. It was not uncommon for them to spend an hour on the phone several nights a week. Although there was no immorality (yet), Jerry found himself fantasizing about Darla. Needless to say the relationship was starting to strain Jerry's relationship with his wife as well. He wanted to know what to do.

I told him that he must end the friendship with Darla immediately—no more lunches and no more phone conversations. He began to protest how painful it would be to end what had become a satisfying friendship for both Darla and himself. I told him that was all the more reason he must end the relationship now. He was playing with fire. I reminded him of Proverbs 6:27: "Can a man take fire in his bosom, and his clothes not be burned?"

Such radical changes are painful in the short-term. But they are well worth the hurt when compared to the consequences of immoral behavior.

3. Visualize the consequences of immoral behavior. My father used to devote the side of our refrigerator to newspaper clippings detailing current scandals of famous personalities. The first thing you would see when coming into our kitchen was this collection of pictures and stories of the rich and famous who had fallen. We nicknamed the collection "Dad's Wall of Shame." Though we laughed about it, there was something healthy about seeing a daily reminder of the consequences of sin.

Earlier, I stated that sin is pleasurable and satisfying—for the moment. Yet there are physical, emotional, and spiritual consequences of sin that we rarely hear told. That is by design. Satan is a liar and a deceiver (see John 8:44) and would rather we not know about the effects of sin.

But Paul reminded us of the consequences of sensual conduct in verse 6: "For it is on account of these things that the wrath of God will come." The term "wrath of God" refers primarily to the coming judgment of God upon unbelievers. Such a judgment is not the result of God's uncontrollable violent temper, but is the natural consequence of His holy nature.

If God's nature demands that He act in such a drastic manner against sin in the lives of unbelievers, should we think that He can overlook sin in the lives of those who are called His children? Christians do not have to face the wrath of God, but they do face His discipline in this life: "For those whom the Lord loves He disciplines, and He scourges every son whom He receives" (Heb. 12:6). And such discipline is never pleasant!

4. Learn to be content with God's provisions in every area of life. As stated before, greed is an obsession with having more and is tantamount to idolatry. It is based on the false assumption that things or people can fill the God-shaped vacuum inside each of us. Greed also stems from the belief that God has short-changed us in some way. If only we had . . .

more money
a different job
a more attractive spouse

Then, we would be truly satisfied. Such assumptions lead us to pursue things outside of God's will for our lives and to fall into all kinds of sin. Look at the relationship between greed and sin found in 1 Timothy 6:9–10: "But those who want to get rich fall into temptation and a snare and many foolish and harmful desires which plunge men into ruin and destruction. For the love of money is *a root of all sorts of evil, and some by longing for it have wandered away from the faith, and pierced themselves with many a pang*" (emphasis mine).

As long as you are living in obedience to God, you have everything you need for a satisfying life. Psalm 84:11 promises that God withholds no good thing from those who walk uprightly. Your job, your bank account, your marital status, your spouse are all part of God's sovereign plan for your life—a plan that was designed for your ultimate happiness and God's glory. Such a realization is the first line of defense against immorality.

If you are heavenly-minded—if your primary desire is to be like Jesus Christ—it does not mean you will be exempt from temptation. It does mean, however, that when temptation comes you will be able to deal decisively with it because of your participation in the death and resurrection of Christ.

✳

ACTION STEPS

1. Identify anything that you have read, seen, or heard in the last week that has fueled immoral thoughts in your life. _____

_____

_____

_____

2. What steps can you take to eliminate those stimuli from your life? _____

_____

_____

_____

3. What relationships do you have that could be potentially dangerous? Discuss those relationships with your spouse. _____

_____

_____

_____

4. Think of someone you know who has fallen into immorality. What have been the consequences of that person's fall? _____

_____

_____

_____

5. List four things that you believe could really make you happy in life. _____

_____

_____

_____

Now, substitute each of those items for the word *greed* in Colossians 3:5.

6. Memorize Colossians 3:5–7.

F O U R

How to Dress for Success

"Robert, I have some bad news for you. The contract on your house has fallen through again." Understandably, these were not welcomed words from my realtor one Monday morning—especially since this was the third contract that had been canceled on a rental property I was trying to unload. (I was beginning to understand my grandfather's adage: "If you *really* hate someone and want to get even with them, give them a rent house!") The realtor continued, "In my twenty years in the business, I have never had a contract fall through for this reason."

My curiosity was piqued. "What happened?"

"Last Saturday night the husband flew into a rage and bludgeoned his wife to death. They found her unrecognizable remains in the back bedroom."

The next day, I received an envelope in the mail. When I opened it, I was shocked to see the contract that this

46

husband and wife had signed earlier on the day of the murder. It was an eerie reminder of the unpredictability of anger that is not kept in check. Earlier in the day that husband and wife were getting along well enough to make a decision to purchase a home. Yet, later in the day, unresolved anger grabbed hold of that man's emotions and caused him to extinguish the life of his partner.

Ralph Waldo Emerson observed that "anger, like fire, finally dies out—after leaving a path of destruction." Anger is also like an acid—it damages both the container in which it is stored and the object on which it is poured. That is why Paul urged those who are "seeking the things above" to learn to deal correctly with this potentially dangerous emotion.

If you are heavenly-minded—that is, if your chief pursuit in life is to conform your affections, attitudes, and actions to the image of Jesus Christ—there are going to be some visible changes in your life right now. In the last chapter, we examined sensual attitudes and actions that a heavenly-minded Christian is to put to death. A person who is seeking the things above is going to deal decisively with sensuality. He or she will seek to eradicate immorality, impurity, evil thoughts, passion, and the root cause—greed—from his or her life.

Although sins of immorality may involve other people, they are basically internal sins. But the next list of negative behaviors found in Colossians 3 involves actions and attitudes against others. Specifically, Paul is going to deal with sins of anger and speech. (We will deal with speech in the next chapter.)

G. Campbell Morgan once referred humorously to these vices as "the sins in good standing."[1] True, we do not hear as many sermons about anger and slander as we do about immorality and impurity. But these sins are just as rampant as the others—and are every bit as unacceptable in the life of one who is trying to become like Jesus Christ.

THE EFFECTS OF OUR TEMPER

It's Time for a Change!

Paul's remedy for sensual behavior was to kill it. But Paul employed a different metaphor about the sins of temper and the tongue. He said we are to "put them all aside" (3:8). He identified these six sins as characteristic of the old self which has been "laid aside" (3:9).

What does Paul mean by "laying aside"? When explaining our actions toward sensual behavior, Paul used the imagery of the death of Jesus Christ. Just as Christ dealt a death blow to sin, we are to put to death certain behavior. But in these verses, Paul was alluding to the resurrection of Christ. Although an editor might scold Paul for mixing his metaphors, the image is nevertheless a powerful one.

When Jesus Christ was raised from the dead, He left His old grave clothes behind. When Peter and John entered the empty tomb, the first thing they noticed were the grave clothes of Jesus Christ that had been left behind:

> Simon Peter therefore also came, following him, and entered the tomb; and he beheld the linen wrappings lying there, and the face-cloth, which had been on His head, not lying with the linen wrappings, but rolled up in a place by itself. So the other disciple who had first come to the tomb entered then also, and saw and believed. (John 20:6–8)

Notice those last four words: "and saw and believed." The evidence that convinced these two disciples that Jesus had truly been raised from the dead was the clothing left behind. They knew these garments had been on the body of Christ. If thieves had stolen the body, they would not have taken the time to unwrap and leave them neatly folded. The only explanation was resurrection. Jesus had exchanged His old garments for those befitting His new body.

In the same way, Paul says that those who have been raised up with Christ to a new quality of life should leave behind the old actions and attitudes that were characteristic of their old nature and put on those attitudes and actions that are consistent with their new life in Christ. Such "laying aside" and "putting on" is the essence of being heavenly-minded. And it is the most powerful evidence to an unbelieving world of the truth of the resurrection.

Don't Get Mad . . . Let God Get Even!

The first three sins Paul mentioned dealt with temper. Although we often use the words *anger, wrath*, and *malice* interchangeably, they are different. *Anger* comes from a Greek word (*orge*) which refers to a smoldering, persistent, negative emotion toward another person. It is distinguished from *wrath* which is a temporary eruption of that emotion.

The long-term physical effects of unresolved anger are well-known. Anger decreases the lymphocytes in our bodies, which results in decreased antibodies to ward off infectious diseases. In their book *Happiness Is a Choice*, Christian psychiatrists Frank Minirth and Paul Meier make this claim: "Pent-up anger is probably the leading cause of death."[2] Anger always demands an expression.

Anger sometimes expresses itself through *wrath*. The word *wrath* comes from the Greek word *thymon* which can also be translated "rage." We speak of people going into a "blind rage." Pent-up anger is like water behind a dam. When the pressure becomes too great, the dam cracks and the water gushes forth uncontrollably. And usually, the damage is irreparable.

Malice is a more subtle expression of anger. This word describes a feeling of ill will toward another. Malice is an emotion that secretly longs to see another person suffer. Although this emotion usually runs underground, it will surface at any opportunity. A person who is filled with malice will take advantage of any opportunity to harm his enemy through speech or action. He rejoices when his enemy suffers misfortune and despairs when his enemy prospers.

Rabbi Harold Kushner illustrates the effects of malice in his book *When Bad Things Happen to Good People* with a story about two shopkeepers who had been bitter rivals for years. Their stores were located across the street from one another. They would spend their days standing in the front door of their shops, keeping an eye on the other's customers. If one of the shopkeepers got a customer, he would smile at his rival in triumph. One night an angel appeared to one of the shopkeepers and said, "God has sent me to teach you a lesson about loving your neighbor. God will grant you anything you ask for, but whatever you get, your competitor will get twice as much. You can ask for money, but whatever you receive, he will receive twice as much. You can ask for health, but he will be twice as healthy. You can ask for a long life, but his will be twice as long. You can ask for children, but he will have twice as many children."

The man frowned, thought for a moment, and said, "All right, strike me blind in one eye!"[3]

Paul is saying that attitudes and actions such as anger, wrath, and malice have no place in the life of one who is heavenly-minded. But how do you "lay aside" such natural emotions?

Dealing with the Root

If wrath and malice are manifestations of anger, then it seems reasonable to assume that the way to stop violent outbursts of rage and feelings of ill will toward others is to deal with the root problem of anger. Just look at some of the Scripture passages dealing with anger:

Cease from anger, and forsake wrath. (Ps. 37:8)

A hot-tempered man stirs up strife, but the slow to anger pacifies contention. (Prov. 15:18)

Wrath is fierce and anger is a flood. (Prov. 27:4)

Scorners set a city aflame, but wise men turn away anger. (Prov. 29:8)

For the churning of milk produces butter, and pressing the nose brings forth blood; so the churning of anger produces strife. (Prov. 30:33)

Be angry, and yet do not sin; do not let the sun go down on your anger, and do not give the devil an opportunity. (Eph. 4:26–27)

This you know, my beloved brethren. But let everyone be quick to hear, slow to speak and slow to anger; for the anger of man does not achieve the righteousness of God. (Jas. 1:19–20)

Is Anger *Always* Wrong?

The answer to that question is obvious to any student of the Bible. The Word of God often speaks of the anger of the Lord. In the last chapter we looked at Colossians 3:6 that speaks of "the wrath of God" (the word translated "wrath" is the Greek word *orge*—anger). Contrary to popular opinion, Jesus Christ was not a mealymouthed Milquetoast who never raised His voice at anyone. Consider His reaction to finding the moneychangers in the temple: "And Jesus entered the temple and cast out all those who were buying and selling in the temple, and overturned the tables of the moneychangers and the seats of those who were selling doves" (Matt. 21:12).

The Lord also was not hesitant to express His outrage against the Pharisees. Remember His scathing words to these legalists in Matthew 23? "Woe to you, scribes and Pharisees, hypocrites, because you shut off the kingdom of heaven from men; for you do not enter in yourselves, nor do you allow those who are entering to go in" (v. 13).

Yes, if we are heavenly-minded there will be times that we are justifiably angry, just as Christ was. But notice that Jesus' anger was never triggered by His own mistreatment. Instead, the only time He became angry was when God was being dishonored or others were being wronged. That is what righteous indignation is all about.

Unfortunately, most of our anger is not righteous, but selfish. Examine the root cause of your anger, and you will discover that it often has to do with your rights being violated. All of us have a list of expectations that we want other people to meet. And when those needs are not met, we become angry.

For example, have you ever been stuck behind a driver on the highway going 50 MPH and become enraged? What is the source of that anger? You believe you have a right to travel 65 MPH, and someone is interfering with that right.

That list of expectations extends into every area of life. We have expectations about our jobs. Some employees feel that they have a right to an automatic pay raise every year. If they do not get a raise, they become angry.

Most husbands and wives have expectations of their mate. Janet grew up in a home where her father was the resident handyman. If there was a leaky faucet, he fixed it. If there was a clogged drain, he unclogged it. Understandably, Janet expected the same thing from her husband, Roger. But Roger had a different solution to household problems: the Yellow Pages. His attitude was, "Why do the work myself when there are legions of trained professionals who can do the work for me?" Janet's anger over "wasting money" on simple repairs was rooted in her unmet expectations.

Church members have certain expections of their pastor. I have a friend who pastors a small church in a county seat town. He followed a popular pastor who was greatly admired in the community. But for some reason the church did not warm up to the new pastor. After about a year, many of the men in the church became openly hostile toward him. What was the source of their anger? The new pastor discovered that his predecessor had gone to the local coffee shop for breakfast every morning—something he had never done. The men enjoyed this informal time with their pastor. The new pastor, unaware of this custom, failed to meet their expectations about what a pastor should be doing in the morning, and they reacted negatively.

One of the most vivid illustrations in the Bible of anger caused by unmet expectations is found in the story of the prodigal son. You remember the story. The younger son asked his father for his portion of the inheritance. After moving to a distant city and squandering his wealth, the boy returned home, broken and contrite. The father was understandably thrilled to receive his younger son back. He ordered a gala celebration to be held in the boy's honor. But notice the older son's response to the situation:

> But he became *angry*, and was not willing to go in; and his father came out and began entreating him. But he answered and said to his father, "Look! For so many years I have been serving you, and I have never neglected a command of yours; and yet you have never given me a kid, that I might be merry with my friends; but when this son of yours came, who has devoured your wealth with harlots, you killed the fattened calf for him." (Luke 15:28–30; emphasis mine)

The source of the older brother's anger was unmet expectations, perceived rights that were violated. He had been diligent and felt that he deserved to be rewarded by his father. When the recognition did not come to him, but went instead to his wayward brother, he felt cheated.

Six Steps for Conquering Anger

How should we handle anger? Thomas Jefferson once wrote, "When angry, count ten before you speak; if very angry, a hundred." Years later, Mark Twain offered a slight revision to Jefferson's words: "When angry, count four. When very angry, swear."[4]

While those suggestions may offer temporary relief, they provide no real lasting solution. Let me suggest six steps that will help you control the destructive emotion of anger.

1. Ignore petty disagreements. My brother is a policeman in a large city, and he sees the seamy side of people's behavior. While that is to be expected in his line of work, it is still discouraging to him. As a pastor, I too see the dark side of people's behavior, and it is very disheartening. Especially among so-called mature Christians. One Sunday morning, a woman caught me after the morning worship service and nearly blew a gasket. Why? Someone had taken "her parking space" that morning. She was so angry she said that she "almost went home and took my money with me!" And stories like that could be repeated a thousand times.

In the last chapter we saw that we need to guard our minds against immoral thoughts. I said that we can choose which thoughts to dwell on and which to ignore. The same can be said about disagreements with others. It is impossible to go through a day without having someone offend you. But *you* choose whether to meditate on that offense or ignore it. A wise person refuses to be conquered by pettiness.

> The beginning of strife is like letting out water, so abandon the quarrel before it breaks out. (Prov. 17:14)
>
> A man's discretion makes him slow to anger, and it is his glory to overlook a transgression. (Prov. 19:11)

A doctor friend once told me that if people understood what happens to them physiologically when they become angry—the poisonous toxins that were released in their bloodstream and the pressure on their circulatory system—they would be more inclined to learn to control their anger and dismiss petty disagreements.

2. Resolve disagreements with others immediately. If a situation arises that you are unable to dismiss, then deal positively with it. Remember, the goal in controlling anger is to keep it from erupting into wrath or smoldering through malice.

Anger is like a headache; it is a sign that something else is wrong. In Ephesians 4:26–27 Paul encouraged us to deal positively with anger, before the day is over: "Be angry, and yet do not sin; do not let the sun go down on your anger, and do not give the devil an opportunity." Someone has said, "He who goes to bed angry has the devil for a bedfellow. Never take your enemies to bed with you!"

If you have a disagreement with someone, take care of it before the day is over. Don't assume that the problem will resolve itself, or that you can deal with it later. It will only intensify. This is especially true with a family member. Never go to bed angry with your spouse or your child. All hostility should be resolved before the lights go out!

3. Ask forgiveness from those you offend with your anger. Are there people whom you have hurt by harsh words: a friend, an employee, your spouse, or your child? Jesus says that you should forget trying to worship until you are reconciled to that person. "If therefore you are presenting your offering at the altar, and there remember that your brother has something against you, leave your offering there before the altar, and go your way; first be reconciled to your brother, and then come and present your offering" (Matt. 5:23–24). Although asking forgiveness may be difficult, it will restore your relationship with that person and with God. You will also discover that a commitment to asking forgiveness from those we offend will also be a strong deterrent against uncontrolled anger. I was reminded of that truth several months ago.

Our church was hosting a major event we had been working toward for months. Several thousand people from our community would attend, including hundreds of potential new members for our church. About thirty minutes before the program was to begin, I walked through the building, making sure every detail had been covered. When I walked into the sanctuary I noticed that the section where our special guests were to be seated was not roped off, as I had instructed. When I looked for the staff member in charge, he was nowhere to be found. Later, I learned that he had gone home early instead of taking care of his responsibility. When he finally returned to church, about five minutes before the program began, I erupted and gave him a piece of my mind I could not afford to lose!

As I looked at him throughout the program, I could tell that I had injured his spirit. I kept arguing with myself that I had every right to be angry—he had been negligent in his duty, he had demonstrated an apathetic attitude, etc. Yet I knew I had wronged him with such a violent outburst. I had difficulty sleeping that night. The next morning I summoned up all of my humility and called him to apologize for the way I had treated him.

However, not only did my apology restore my relationship with the staff member, but it has made me more hesitant to lose my temper. Knowing that I will have to ask forgiveness later for my angry outbursts is a powerful incentive to keep my temper in check!

4. Refuse to associate with angry people. Anger is a learned response. In my experience, most people who have trouble controlling their tempers come from homes where one or both parents had the same problem. We cannot control our heritage but we *can* control our friends. Psalm 1 commands us to refuse to associate with the ungodly, lest we become influenced by them: "Oh, the joys of those who do not follow evil men's advice, who do not hang around with sinners, scoffing at the things of God" (Ps. 1:1, TLB).

In the same way, Proverbs 22:24–25 warns against our associating with angry people, lest we mimic their ways: "Do not associate with a man given to anger; or go with a hot-tempered man, lest you learn his ways, and find a snare for yourself."

5. Learn to differentiate between rights and responsibilities. The chief source of anger is unmet expectations. To eliminate anger we must learn to give up our rights. However, it is important that we differentiate between our rights and our responsibilities. We are to give up our rights, but never our responsibilities.

For example, consider the above illustration regarding my outburst at the staff member. My anger was triggered by an unmet expectation—the staff member failed to fulfill an assignment. Should I have given up that expectation and allowed him to perform however he chose? No, that expectation is not a right but a responsibility. As pastor of the church, the congregation holds me responsible for the performance of the staff. I would be shirking my duties if I failed to have standards for employees of the church. My mistake was in how I corrected the staff member.

Likewise, you have certain responsibilities that should not be confused with rights. For example, you have a responsibility to discipline your children. You cannot "give up" that responsibility. When they misbehave, you have a duty to correct them in a loving, but firm way—even if their misbehavior also involves one of your rights. My sister-in-law has a rule that her children cannot come into her bedroom before 7:00 A.M., even if they arise early. When they disobey that rule, they are punished. Even though there is a self-serving purpose behind that rule, she still has the parental responsibility to enforce that rule.

You also have a responsibility to admonish fellow Christians when they sin in such a way as to hurt the church. Admittedly, this can be confusing. If a Christian sins against me, what is to be my response? Peter asked the Lord the same question in Matthew 18:21. Jesus replied that we should forgive an offending brother an unlimited number of times. To forgive literally means "to let go of." However, Jesus drew a distinction between personal and corporate offenses. When a Christian is involved in sin that hurts his own life or the body of Christ as a whole, we are to lovingly rebuke that believer (see Matt. 18:15-20).

6. *Transfer your rights to God.* If we are indeed going to be heavenly-minded, it means we must turn over our personal rights and expectations to God in the same way that Jesus Christ did. Jesus' attitude about His rights is clearly expressed in Philippians 2:5–8:

> Have this attitude in yourselves which was also in Christ Jesus, who, although He existed in the form of God, did not regard equality with God a thing to be grasped, but emptied Himself, taking the form of a bond-servant, and being made in the likeness of men. And being found in appearance as a man, He humbled Himself by becoming obedient to the point of death, even death on a cross.

Think for a moment about your expectations of other people in your life—we all have them. What is it that you expect from your spouse, employer, church, or friends? Are you willing to transfer those rights to God?

By suggesting that we transfer those rights to God, I am not suggesting that we should be dishonest with ourselves and pretend we have no expectations:

If my husband doesn't want to take out the garbage,
that is fine with me.

If my wife wants me to watch a movie with her instead of
"Monday Night Football," I don't really care.

If my boss changes my vacation days,
I'll be happy to oblige him.

If my friend does not invite me to his dinner party,
I'll be content to stay at home.

"Transferring our rights to God" deals with our response when our rights are violated. A person who has emptied himself of his rights is not a robot, void of any feelings. Instead, when his expectations are not met, he acknowledges that he has been genuinely hurt. But instead of trying to avenge his offense through a violent outburst of wrath or long-term malice, he turns his case over to God. And he expects God to judge the situation fairly.

Jesus Christ showed us how to respond to offenses from others: "And while being reviled, He did not revile in return; while suffering, He uttered no threats, but kept entrusting Himself to Him who judges righteously" (1 Pet. 2:23). With a simple word or a nod to heaven, Christ could have annihilated His enemies. Yet He chose to let God take care of the situation.

You may be thinking, *Of course Jesus could respond in that way. He is God.* Yes, His response was supernatural—no doubt about it. Yet Paul's argument in Colossians 3 is that we are capable of the same response because of our participation in the death and resurrection of Jesus Christ. If our hearts and minds are centered on the things above, we too can transfer our rights and expectations to God and eliminate the root cause of anger. Turn your rights over to God and live a happier—and longer—life!

✳

ACTION STEPS

1. Describe a recent experience in which you became angry. _____
_____
_____
_____

2. What "right" or "expectation" was at the root of your anger in the above incident? _____

3. Identify your expectations of the following people:
Your spouse: _____
_____

Your children: _____
_____

Your employer: _____
_____

Your best friend: _____
_____

4. Would you be willing to turn those expectations over to God? Take a moment to pray and commit these expectations to God.

5. Is there someone from whom you need to ask forgiveness for an outburst of anger? _____
_____

6. Memorize the following verses: Ephesians 4:26–27 and James 1:19–20.

Speech Therapy 101

In an interview several years ago, former talk-show host Johnny Carson was asked about any regrets he had concerning his career. He responded, "I suppose one regret I have is some of the things I have said on the air. I hadn't planned to say them; the words just slipped out. I would give anything if I could retrieve some of those words."[1] Has that ever happened to you? Can you recall words you have spoken in anger, in jest, or in idle conversation that you instantly regretted and wished you could retrieve? I certainly can.

Years ago when I was a youth minister, I was presiding over our senior recognition service at our church. That day all of our graduating seniors and their parents gathered together for this special service. It was a somber mood as parents contemplated sending their children off to school. So I thought a little humor might be appreciated. I began my remarks by saying, "Having been here for seven years now, it is rewarding for me to see our young people graduate from high school, go off to college, marry, and have children—though not always in that order." Everyone laughed—almost everyone. No sooner had the words fallen from my lips than I remembered that one of our seniors had just had a baby out of wedlock and, in spite of the understandable embarrassment, had continued to come to church.

I saw the mother and daughter get up and leave; the girl was in tears. I was absolutely horrified. How could I have said such a thing and forgotten about this girl's circumstances? I went to see the girl and her mother. Fortunately, the mom was very understanding and said she knew that I did not have her daughter in mind when I spoke. In time, the girl did come back to church. But the incident was a painful reminder to me of how potentially destructive our words are.

The Bible is filled with warnings about controlling our speech:

> The one who guards his mouth preserves his life; the one who opens wide his lips comes to ruin. (Prov. 13:3)

> A gentle answer turns away wrath, but a harsh word stirs up anger. (Prov. 15:1)

> The words of a whisperer are like dainty morsels, and they go down into the innermost parts of the body. (Prov. 18:8)

> If anyone thinks himself to be religious, and yet does not bridle his tongue but deceives his own heart, this man's religion is worthless. (Jas. 1:26)

> Let him who means to love life and see good days refrain his tongue from evil and his lips from speaking guile. (1 Pet. 3:10)

Just as one careless spark can ravage hundreds of thousands of acres of a forest, so one word can destroy the

Truth told with the intention of hurting another person is slander. When Claude Pepper from Florida was running for senator in 1950, one of his opponents attacked him as follows: "Are you aware that Claude Pepper is known all over Washington as a shameless extrovert? He also practiced nepotism with his sister-in-law, and has a sister who once was a thespian in wicked New York City. Worst of all, before his marriage he habitually practiced celibacy!"[3]

Why does Paul urge Christians to lay aside slander?

1. Slander is divisive. As we will see in a moment, those who are heavenly-minded are intent on creating unity among believers, not disunity. And nothing separates friends, family, or churches more than slander. As we saw in Proverbs 16:28: "A perverse man spreads strife, and a slanderer separates intimate friends."

2. Slander necessitates our making judgments about other people we are not qualified to make. When we slander someone, we assume that they *deserve* to have their reputation put to death, and we assume the role of public executioner. But the Bible clearly says that we are not to make final judgments about anyone—that is God's business. "Do not speak against one another, brethren. He who speaks against a brother, or judges his brother, speaks against the law, and judges the law; but if you judge the law, you are not a doer of the law, but a judge of it. There is only one Lawgiver and Judge, the One who is able to save and to destroy; but who are you who judge your neighbor?" (Jas. 4:11–12).

The Bible draws a distinction between discernment and judgment. Jesus said we are not to judge another: "Do not judge lest you be judged" (Matt. 7:1). The word translated "judge" here and in James 4:11 is the Greek word *krino*, which carries the idea of condemnation. It refers to passing a final sentence on someone that does not allow for their repentance. When we engage in that type of judgment, our motives are usually transparent. We are attempting to elevate ourselves at the expense of another person.

A successful businessman I know is a constant target of criticism. Other Christians constantly bombard him with all kinds of attacks: he is arrogant, he is manipulative, he is materialistic, and so on. Maybe some of the criticism is justified. But their motivation in making such judgments is not out of a deep concern for him—if it were, they would confront him in a loving, but firm manner. Instead, their criticism appears to be motivated by jealousy.

On the other hand, there are times when we must evaluate another's actions. For example, maybe you are a manager who is interviewing someone for a job. You must evaluate whether that person is qualified for the job. You must make a judgment. Or, maybe you are a single adult and you are deciding whether or not to date a certain individual. As a dedicated Christian, you have decided to date only those who have a similar commitment to Christ. That means making a judgment about another person's spirituality. Possibly you have had the experience of serving on a jury. You must render a judgment about the person on trial.

Judgments are a part of everyday life. But those judgments should always be motivated by a desire to help another person, rather than harm them or promote yourself. In 1 Corinthians 6:5, Paul lamented that there were not some in the Corinthian congregation who were capable of making wise judgments about others instead of relying on the pagan courts to settle disputes: "I say this to your shame. Is it so, that there is not among you one wise man who will be able to decide between his brethren?" The word translated "decide" in that passage is *diakrino*, which means "to discern." Someone in the church should have been capable of a sound judgment. While a heavenly-minded person is not to condemn another person, he should be able make sound judgments.

There is only one legitimate reason to share damaging information about another person, and that is if your ultimate goal is to restore that person to a right relationship with God. If that is your motive, then you should always be willing to go to that person and confront him with the information: "And if your brother sins, go and reprove him in private; if he listens to you, you have won your brother" (Matt. 18:15).

3. Slander causes irreparable damage. Once a word is spoken it can never be retrieved. And once a reputation is ruined by slander, it can never be restored. I remember years ago when Labor Secretary Raymond Donovan was indicted by a grand jury and ultimately exonerated after a lengthy court battle. As he left the courtroom, a reporter asked him what he was going to do. Donovan replied, "Which office do I go to get my reputation back?"[4]

The story is told of a young man during the Middle Ages who confessed to a monk, "I've sinned by telling slanderous statements about someone. What should I do now?" The monk replied, "Put a feather on every doorstep in town." The young man did just that. He then came back to the monk wondering if there was anything else that he should do. The monk instructed, "Go back and pick up all those feathers." The young man replied excitedly, "That's impossible! By now the wind will have blown them all over town!" Said the monk, "So has your slanderous word become impossible to retrieve."

Abusive Speech

The next type of speech that we are to lay aside if we are heavenly-minded is translated "abusive speech" in the *New American Standard Version*. The *New International Version* translates the word "filthy language." Remember Paul's premise—wrong attitudes toward others manifest themselves through our speech. One way we express our negative emotions toward another person is through slander. But another way we demonstrate an uncaring or hardened attitude toward someone is by assaulting them with obscene speech or with dirty jokes.

Some people derive a perverse pleasure from bombarding their more morally sensitive friends with vulgar speech—just to see what kind of reaction they get. I heard a story on the radio last week (which was the basis for an episode on a popular television program) about a woman who fainted every time one of her coworkers used obscene or suggestive language. You can imagine the "fun" her work associates had with her. She sued her coworkers because of their harassment and won her case. Her rights had been violated.

True, most people don't react that viscerally to obscene speech. Nevertheless, when we engage in that kind of speech, we are verbally "abusing" that person and revealing our disdain for his or her rights. A heavenly-minded person seeks to edify rather than destroy another person by his speech: "Let no unwholesome word proceed from your mouth, but only such a word as is good for edification according to the need of the moment, that it may give grace to those who hear" (Eph. 4:29).

Lying

Another form of destructive speech that Paul commanded us to lay aside is lying. Nothing destroys a relationship any faster than dishonesty. Ask most people to recall the break-up of an important relationship and identify the root cause of the disintegration of that relationship, and they will usually say dishonesty.

And yet, as hurtful as lies are, most of us consciously choose to lie every day. In their book *The Day America Told the Truth*, authors James Patterson and Peter Kim surveyed two thousand Americans about the most intimate aspects of their morality. The chapter entitled "American Liars" caught my attention:

> Just about everyone lies—91 percent of us lie regularly. The majority of us find it hard to get through a week without lying. One in five can't make it through a single day—and we're talking about conscious, premeditated lies. In fact, the way some people talk about trying to do without lies, you'd think that they were smokers trying to get through a day without a cigarette. . . . We lie to just about everyone, and the better we know someone, the likelier we are to have told them a serious lie."[5]

As rampant as lying is in our culture, it is still unacceptable in the life of someone who is heavenly-minded. Take a moment and look at two passages of Scripture that reveal God's attitude about lies. Proverbs 6:16–19 lists the seven sins God hates most. Notice that two of them have to do with lying: "There are six things which the Lord hates, yes, seven which are an abomination to Him: haughty eyes, *a lying tongue*, and hands that shed innocent blood, a heart that devises wicked plans, feet that run rapidly to evil, *a false witness who utters lies*, and one who spreads strife among brothers (emphasis mine)."

Another powerful demonstration of God's attitude toward lying is found in the story of Ananias and Sapphira, the couple in the early church who lied about some property they had sold: "But Peter said, 'Ananias, why has Satan filled your heart to lie to the Holy Spirit, and to keep back some of the price of the land? . . . You have not lied to men, but to God.' And as he heard these words, Ananias fell down and breathed his last; and great fear came upon all who heard of it" (Acts 5:3–5).

God hates lying because it is the very antithesis of His nature. Jesus said, "I am the way, and the truth, and the life" (John 14:6). On the other hand consider how Jesus described Satan in John 8:44: "He was a murderer from the beginning, and does not stand in the truth, because there is no truth in him. Whenever he speaks a lie, he speaks from his own nature; for he is a liar, and the father of lies." Thus, when a Christian lies, he is behaving like a child of Satan. That is why Paul urged the heavenly-minded person to strip off the old habit of lying.

CONTROLLING THE "BEAST" IN YOUR MOUTH

Is it possible to rid our speech of slander, off-color remarks, and lying? James 3:8 reminds us of the difficulty of controlling our speech: "But no one can tame the tongue; it is a restless evil and full of deadly poison." However, the same James tells us that if we don't control our speech, our religion is worthless: "If anyone thinks himself to be religious, and yet does not bridle his tongue but deceives his own heart, this man's religion is worthless" (Jas. 1:26).

Let me share with you seven helpful suggestions for laying aside these natural, yet destructive, kinds of speech:

1. Realize the eternal consequences of your speech. Did you know that Jesus said that all of us will one day give an account of *every word* we have ever spoken? (For some, that may consume most of eternity!) "And I say to you, that every careless word that men shall speak, they shall render account for it in the day of judgment. For by your words you shall be justified, and by your words you shall be condemned" (Matt. 12:36–37).

How will it be possible to be judged by every word we have spoken? Scientists tell us that the sound waves set in motion by our voices go on an endless journey through space. If we had instruments delicate enough and the power to stand upon some planet long years afterward, we might be able to hear the words we spoke long ago. Can you imagine having every word you have ever spoken played back? God has that ability. Such a realization should be a strong encouragement to control our speech.

2. Meditate on Scripture passages dealing with speech. Memorizing and meditating on God's thoughts about our speech can be a powerful deterrent from engaging in slander, filthy communication, and lying. Let me suggest several verses you might want to start with:

The one who guards his mouth preserves his life; the one who opens wide his lips comes to ruin. (Prov. 13:3)

Do you see a man who is hasty in his words? There is more hope for a fool than for him. (Prov. 29:20)

Let no unwholesome word proceed from your mouth, but only such a word as is good for edification according to the need of the moment, that it may give grace to those who hear. (Eph. 4:29)

If anyone thinks himself to be religious, and yet does not bridle his tongue but deceives his own heart, this man's religion is worthless. (Jas. 1:26)

3. Refuse to criticize another person until you have confronted him or her personally. If indeed you are "discerning" rather than "judging" another person, you will always want to deal with him or her personally. That means that we should refuse to listen to gossip and slander. Anytime someone wants to share some "information" about another, you should ask, "Have you talked to that person about this yet?" or "Do you mind if I quote you on that?" It's amazing what a silencing effect those questions have! If we would refuse to listen to gossips, they would stop.

4. Abstain from all exaggerations, distortions, and lies. We all use exaggeration or distortion of the truth in our speech.

How many times have you been arguing with your spouse and said, "You always . . . "? Such a statement may provide emphasis for your point, but it probably is not accurate. Our mate doesn't *always* do anything! Or have you ever said to your child, "You never do what I tell you to do"? Again, an exaggeration of the truth. There was probably *some* time when your child obeyed you.

Sometimes we distort or twist the facts to suit our need. There may be a kernel of truth in what we are saying, but it is difficult to find in the pile of . . . well, lies! Calvin Miller, a professor at Southwestern Baptist Theological Seminary, tells the following story.

> Many years ago I worked my way through seminary employed in a factory. During final exams one semester, I knew that if I was going to pass a test the next day I must study and not go to work. Yet, I didn't want to lie to my boss about why I wasn't showing up for work that night. I hit upon this plan. My wife and I were going to have fish for dinner. So I laid down in bed and asked her to bring me the package of frozen fish we were going to eat. Then, as I remained in a prone position, I threw the fish into the air, caught them, returned them to my wife, and told her to call my boss. "Tell him that I'm flat on my back in bed and had just thrown up my dinner," I said. It worked. I did not have to go to work that night. But was that "speaking the truth in love"? [6]

Distortions and exaggerations are the first cousins of lying—but they have the same end result. We are to lay aside *all* falsehoods from our speech.

5. When in doubt, keep silent. Former White House spokesman Larry Speaks gave this word of advice to incoming White House spokesman Marlin Fitzwater, "Remember, you don't have to explain what you don't say." The Bible also extols the value of silence:

> A prudent man conceals knowledge, but the heart of fools proclaims folly. (Prov. 12:23)

He who restrains his words has knowledge and he who has a cool spirit is a man of understanding. Even a fool, when he keeps silent, is considered wise. When he closes his lips, he is counted prudent. (Prov. 17:27–28)

He who guards his mouth and his tongue, guards his soul from troubles. (Prov. 21:23)

This you know, my beloved brethren. But let everyone be quick to hear, slow to speak and slow to anger. (Jas. 1:19)

6. Purify your heart through positive input. Jesus reminds us that our speech is simply an indication of what is in our heart: "For the mouth speaks out of that which fills the heart. The good man out of his good treasure brings forth what is good; and the evil man out of his evil treasure brings forth what is evil" (Matt. 12:34–35). If you are having a difficult time with impurity in your life, you may need to rid your life of negative input—magazines, books, television programs, or immoral friends. It is an overused analogy, but it is nevertheless true. Our mind is like a computer—garbage in, garbage out. Therefore, we need to program our minds with the positive input that comes from God's Word: "Finally, brethren, whatever is true, whatever is honorable, whatever is right, whatever is pure, whatever is lovely, whatever is of good repute, if there is any excellence and if anything worthy of praise, let your mind dwell on these things" (Phil. 4:8).

7. Genuinely love other people. Abusive speech that hurts others—slander, filthy communication, and lying—is symptomatic of a hostile attitude toward other people. In Colossians 3:9–11, Paul reminded us that the heavenly-minded person has shed the old behavior patterns of his former life and put on the behavior that becomes our new life in Christ. And then Paul adds a word about our unity as believers: "a renewal in which there is no distinction between the Greek and Jew, circumcised and uncircumcised, barbarian, Scythian, slave and freeman, but Christ is all, and in all." Notice those last three words "and in all."

The Lord Jesus Christ resides in the heart of every believer. And that means when you slander another Christian, you are slandering Christ. It means when you tell a dirty joke to another Christian, you are telling it to Christ. And it means when you lie to another Christian, you are lying to Christ. The heavenly-minded believer is one who measures her or his every word as if she or he were speaking to Christ Himself.

✳

ACTION STEPS

1. Identify the situations in which you are most tempted to gossip about or slander others. _____

_____

_____

2. Which of your friends or work associates are most prone to gossip? Should you separate yourself from these people, if possible? Why or why not? _____

_____

_____

_____

3. Relate an experience where you have seen gossip hurt another person or organization. _____

_____

_____

_____

4. Think through a recent experience in which someone shared damaging information about another person. What was your response? Write out what would have been the best response using the principles we have discussed in this chapter. _____

_____

_____

_____

5. Identify some instances during the last week when you have exaggerated or distorted the truth. _____

_____

_____

6. Ask God to help you control any slanderous, corrupt, or false speech. Memorize and meditate on Colossians 3:8–10; Ephesians 4:29; and James 1:26.

SIX

The Power
of Positive Acting

One of the unique characteristics of the seminary I attended is its dress code—every male is required to wear a coat and tie. Although some students might balk at such a requirement, the seminary has a philosophy behind its standard. The administration believes that ministry is a respectable profession—just as important as banking, real estate, or law. Consequently, those pursuing a career in ministry should dress in a way that is in keeping with their high calling.

Paul makes the same point in Colossians 3. The heavenly-minded Christian should "take off" behavior that is characteristic of the old nature and "put on" behavior that is consistent with the new nature. In the previous two chapters we have examined the actions and attitudes that Christians are to shed: anger, wrath, malice, slander, abusive speech, and lying. But just taking off certain behavior is not enough. We must also put on new actions to replace the old.

Sometimes when my wife and I have been getting ready to go to a party, she has examined my attire and said, "You are not going to wear *that*, are you?" Now, suppose I were to go into the bedroom, take off the offending garments, but not put on anything else. How happy do you think she would be to have me as her escort for the evening? Implicit in her request to remove my old clothes was to put on something *else*.

That concept may seem elementary to you. But it has always amazed me how many people there are who define Christians by what they don't do, rather than by what they do. Many people would describe a heavenly-minded person as one who doesn't break the Ten Commandments, smoke, drink, go to R-rated movies, etc. But I could argue that this book does none of those things; nor does the chair in which you are sitting; nor do the residents of your local cemetery. But who wants to be like a book, a chair, or a corpse?

Yes, the Bible gives certain restrictions about a Christian's behavior. But the distinguishing characteristic of a Christian is not what he doesn't do, but what he does and who he is. A heavenly-minded Christian will work to rid his life of certain actions and attitudes; but at the same time, he will be diligent to put on behavior that is fitting to his heavenly calling. God's purpose for our lives is that we be transformed into the image of His Son (Rom. 8:25–29).

To be transformed into God's image means to change our appearance so that we resemble the Lord Jesus Christ. How is such a change possible? To look like Jesus, we must "dress" like Jesus. And in these verses from Colossians, Paul listed the six "garments" that characterized the life of Christ.

CHARACTERISTICS OF CHRIST

Compassion

The first quality that Paul urged us to clothe ourselves with is compassion, or as the *King James Version* reads, "bowels of mercies." You will remember in chapter 1 that I said ancient writers believed that the center of emotion was not the heart, but the bowels. The bowels were the "gut" of a person. Thus, the word "bowel" (*oiktirmos* in Greek) indicates a deep, gut-level empathy for people that results in positive action.

During World War I, a reporter was watching a Red Cross nurse swab the infected wound of soldier. After watching the sickening sight for a few moments, the reporter said to the nurse, "I would not do what you do for a million dollars." The nurse, looking up at the reporter, replied, "Neither would I." A compassionate person is one who is so moved by the needs and hurts of others that he or she cannot help but respond.

Jesus' life was marked by compassion. The motivation for many of His miracles was His concern for the hurts of others:

> And a leper came to Him, beseeching Him and falling on his knees before Him, and saying to Him, "If You are willing, You can make me clean." And *moved with compassion*, He stretched out His hand and touched him, and said to him, "I am willing; be cleansed." (Mark 1:40–41, emphasis mine)

> And seeing the multitudes, *He felt compassion* for them, because they were distressed and downcast like sheep without a shepherd. (Matt. 9:36, emphasis mine)

Two of Jesus' best-known parables taught the importance of compassion. In the story of the prodigal son, the father is a type of God patiently waiting for the return of his wayward child. Notice the father's initial reaction upon seeing his son: "And he got up and came to his father. But while he was still a long way off, his father saw him, and felt compassion for him, and ran and embraced him, and kissed him" (Luke 15:20).

In the parable of the good Samaritan, Jesus contrasted the indifference of the religious leaders toward an injured man with the compassion shown by a foreigner. The Samaritan, unlike the religious leaders of the day, was genuinely concerned with peoples' needs: "But a certain Samaritan, who was on a journey, came upon him; and when he saw him, he felt compassion, and came to him, and bandaged up his wounds, pouring oil and wine on them; and he put him on his own beast, and brought him to an inn, and took care of him" (Luke 10:33–34).

Are there people in your family, among your friends, in your office, in your church, who have specific needs that you are capable of meeting? Maybe it is a need for money, clothing, or food. Possibly it may be a need for attention, an encouraging word, or just a sympathetic ear. Paul said that if you are a heavenly-minded individual, your life is going to mirror the compassion demonstrated by the Lord Jesus Christ—a compassion that always resulted in positive action.

Kindness

I like the way one lexicographer defines the Greek word for kindness (*chrestotes*): "It was used to describe wine which has grown mellow with age and has lost its harshness."[1] To act kindly toward another person means to deal with him or her from the perspective of grace, not law. It means giving people what they need, rather than what they deserve.

When I was growing up, I always seemed to have more money than my brother, sister, or even my parents. They were always borrowing money from me. By the time I reached the seventh grade, my mom was in debt to me several hundred dollars. (Now that I'm a parent, I can see how easily that could happen!) One day, as she was driving me to school, I said, "Mom, I need some of my money back." She broke into tears and said, "Robert, I don't have any way to pay you the money now." I sat through my first-period class feeling terrible about putting that pressure on my mom. After class, I went to the office, called the school where my mom taught, and left this message, "Mom, you don't owe me anything." Of course, in time, my mom did pay me the money she owed me. But until she died, she often spoke of that act of kindness.

Again, the life of Christ illustrated the quality of kindness. Fortunately, Christ did not give us what we deserved, but what we needed. Out of kindness, He gave up His life for us. "But when *the kindness of God* our Savior and His love for mankind appeared, He saved us, not on the basis of deeds which we have done in righteousness, but according to His mercy, by the washing of regeneration and renewing by the Holy Spirit" (Titus 3:4–5, emphasis mine).

And Paul urged us to exhibit the same kindness to others that Christ showed us: "And be *kind* to one another, tender-hearted, forgiving each other, just as God in Christ also has forgiven you" (Eph. 4:32 emphasis mine).

Are there opportunities you have to demonstrate kindness instead of harshness to others? Husbands, maybe your wife has spent all of her grocery money for the month, and there are still fifteen days left. Although justice might require her to do the best she can the rest of the month, what would be the kind thing to do?

Employers, maybe one of your employees made a mistake that cost your company money. Justice might say the employee should be terminated, but what is the kind thing to do? Parents, suppose your child wrecks the car. Justice would say the child should be grounded for six weeks. But what is the kind thing to do?

Being like Christ doesn't mean that we never act firmly. It means that our first choice—our preferred choice—will always be to deal kindly with others.

Humility

Study the Greek word translated "humility" (*tapinophrosunee*) and you will discover that in the Greek culture this attribute was treated as a vice, not a virtue. Humility was a contemptible quality. For a person to willingly submit to anyone, including God, was a violation of that person's freedom. Yet, in Christianity, humility is extolled as a quality to be cultivated. Look at some of the biblical passages concerning humility:

> When pride comes, then comes dishonor, but with the humble is wisdom. (Prov. 11:2)

> It is better to be of a humble spirit with the lowly, than to divide the spoil with the proud. (Prov. 16:19)

> But to this one I will look, to him who is humble and contrite of spirit, and who trembles at My word. (Isa. 66:2)

> And whoever exalts himself shall be humbled; and whoever humbles himself shall be exalted. (Matt. 23:12)

> And all of you, clothe yourselves with humility toward one another, for God is opposed to the proud, but gives grace to the humble. Humble yourselves, therefore, under the mighty hand of God, that He may exalt you at the proper time. (1 Pet. 5:5–6)

What is humility? It is an attitude that views our accomplishments and our failures from God's perspective. People have a difficult time maintaining a balanced view of themselves. They usually gravitate to one of two extremes: "I am so wonderful, how could God ever get along without me?" or "I am just a lowly worm who can't do anything."

Scripture urges a balanced view of ourselves: "For through the grace given to me I say to every man among you not to think more highly of himself than he ought to think; but to think so as to have sound judgment, as God has allotted to each a measure of faith" (Rom. 12:3).

Let's get practical for a moment. How do you know if you have really put on the garment of humility? A humble person will exhibit four characteristics:

1. *Willing to give other people credit for successes.* A truly humble person has no trouble sharing the spotlight with others. He realizes that whatever success he enjoys in life is a collaborative effort. A wise executive will give credit to his management team for a profitable year; a wise pastor will give credit to his people for their work in building a growing church; and a wise mother will teach her children to thank God for any scholastic honors they receive.

The bottom line of humility is realizing that every good thing in our lives, ultimately, is the result of God's graciousness to us. In 1 Corinthians 4:7, Paul asked an interesting question: "For who regards you as superior? And what do you have that you did not receive? But if you did receive it, why do you boast as if you had not received it?" Your possessions, your children, your position, and your appearance are gifts from God. Such a realization is a powerful antidote to pride.

2. *Refuses to hold on to his or her rights.* When we understand that every good thing in life comes from God, we will stop doggedly clinging to our rights. We will be more interested in accomplishing God's purpose than fulfilling our own agenda. Jesus Christ is the supreme example of One who was willing to give up His divine rights to accomplish God's purpose.

3. *Resists the need to always be right.* After Paul's admonition to have a proper estimation of ourselves (see Rom.

12:3), he discussed the concept of spiritual gifts. God has given each Christian a unique gift. Some have the gift of teaching, others have the gift of mercy, still others have the gift of giving, and so on. With those differing gifts come differing perspectives about a subject.

I think about a couple that came to see me last week. They had a rebellious teenage son who was running with the wrong crowd, playing hooky from school, and habitually breaking his curfew. The husband had the spiritual gift of prophecy. His solution was to throw his son out of the house. The mother had the spiritual gift of mercy. She argued for a more tempered and loving approach to her son's misbehavior. Who was right? Both were. The boy needed to be firmly disciplined (although maybe not in that way). But the discipline needed to be administered in a loving, restorative way.

Rather than trying to force other people to see things your way, appreciate their unique spiritual gifts and perspectives. A humble person realizes that he does not have a corner on the truth. He appreciates and respects the differing gifts and perpectives of others.

4. Demonstrates an interest in serving others. Let's admit it. Most of us tend to value other people in proportion to how they can serve us. We select a mate who we think will meet our physical and emotional needs. We hire employees who will help us fulfill our vocational goals. We choose churches that will meet our spiritual needs. Yet Jesus had a different view of people. People were not to be used, but served. In describing Himself, He said, "The Son of Man did not come to be served, but to serve" (Matt. 20:28).

What a remarkable statement to make! Just think about it for a moment. Jesus Christ is the One who created us (see Col. 1:16). He had the most ambitious and worthy goal of all: to reconcile the world to Himself. Thus, He had every right to view us as instruments to accomplish His purpose; but He did not create us to meet His objectives—He came to fulfill our needs! As Christ's followers, we are to adopt that same attitude about other people.

Let me give you some practical ways to apply this principle. Husbands, you might say to your wives, "Honey, this Saturday I have a few hours off. What can I do around the house to help you?" Or mothers, you might say to your children, "This afternoon after school is yours. Wherever you want to go and whatever you want to do, I'll take you there." Employers, if you want to dumbfound your employees, go into their offices tomorrow morning and say, "I know you have a lot of pressure on you right now. What can I do to help you be more successful in your work?"

All of these characteristics are evident in a heavenly-minded person who has clothed himself with humility.

Gentleness

Two by-products of humility are mentioned next: gentleness and patience. Gentleness is sometimes translated "meekness." Unfortunately, when we think of meekness we think of the similar sounding word weakness. Yet, in reality, the meaning of gentleness or meekness is power that is under control.

One writer notes that this word was used to describe a soothing wind, a healing medicine, and a colt that had been broken. In each case, the power has been harnessed. When I think of this word, I think of the scene from the movie *King Kong* in which the giant ape held the beautiful girl in his hand and began stroking her gently. Now that was power under control!

The heavenly-minded Christian is one who will not let his emotions—especially hostile feelings—overpower him. Instead, he will react the way Christ did on the cross. Instead of lashing out in anger at His enemies or calling down the heavenly hosts to judge them immediately, He said, "Father, forgive them; for they do not know what they are doing" (Luke 23:34).

Patience

The fifth "garment" Paul urged us to clothe ourselves with is "patience." Again, patience flows out of humility. When we see ourselves as God sees us, we should be more able to act with patience toward others.

The word translated "patience" is *makrothumeo*. It means "long-tempered." The word usually refers to people, not circumstances. In the Bible, patience means more than tolerating red lights, delayed flights, or long lines at the supermarket. Patience relates to enduring the mistreatment of others. Chrysostom said, "It is a word which is used of a man who is wronged and who has it easily in his power to avenge himself, but he never does it." The word is antithetical to what the Greeks taught. Aristotle taught that it was a virtue to refuse to tolerate insult and to strike back.[2] We hear the same thing today: "You don't have to be a doormat," or "Don't get mad, get even."

Yet the heavenly-minded person is one who not only endures mistreatment by others, but actually forgives it. Paul went on to say, "Bearing with one another, and forgiving each other, whoever has a complaint against anyone; just as the Lord forgave you, so also should you" (Col. 3:13). The Greek word translated "forgive" means "to release." That is the essence of forgiveness—letting go of people's offenses against us, instead of holding on to them. And why should we do that? Because of God's forgiveness of us. Paul wrote in Ephesians 4:32: "And be kind to one another, tender-hearted, forgiving each other, just as God in Christ also has forgiven you." God forgave us when we did not deserve forgiveness; He forgave us unconditionally. We are to mirror that same forgiveness toward others.

The *Dallas Morning News* carried a story about a woman who learned firsthand about undeserved and unconditional forgiveness. Lori and Douglas White, a newlywed Christian couple, were taking an evening stroll at a nearby junior college. They were excitedly discussing all of the things you might imagine: having children and purchasing a home. Little did they know that in a few moments, an unknown stranger would forever change their lives. A man suddenly accosted them and asked for their money:

> Until the man showed them his gun, neither of the Whites believed they were in danger because they had encountered panhandlers before, she said.
>
> But when he showed the gun, they immediately began praying, which irritated the gunman and prompted him to command, "Yeah, you better pray. Where's your God now?"
>
> Despite the man's taunts, Mrs. White said she and her husband kept praying.
>
> "We were just asking God for forgiveness. Doug said, "'Please don't let him hurt Lori.'"
>
> Mrs. White said her husband could easily have overpowered the smaller man, but he didn't try. He even offered to return to the truck for his wallet, though he had left it at home.
>
> Behaving "real cold," Mrs. White said, the man ordered them to lie on the ground.
>
> "He told us to turn around, and Doug turned toward him. The guy said, 'You looked at me, you shouldn't have done that,'" she said. "He told us to just lay down. He was right behind Doug. I was just a step or two from him."
>
> As she walked toward the grass, she said, her husband abruptly turned to her and, in a raised voice, said, "Run, Lori."
>
> She refused.
>
> "I told him I wasn't leaving him.

"The guy said, 'If you run, I'll blow his ——— head off.' I told Doug I wasn't leaving him."

Mrs. White said the first of two shots came as a surprise.

"I heard Doug say, 'Oh, God, I'm bleeding.'"

Mrs. White declined to discuss details about her attack. She remembers the man pointing the gun at the back of her head, sometimes in her ear, as he assaulted her about sixty feet from where her husband lay dying.

"While I was praying, I had a thought, 'Forgive him,'" she said. "I couldn't understand then why I had that thought. But I understand now."

"Jesus forgave the world when he was crucified," she explained, so He could forgive her attacker.[3]

Lori White is exhibit A of what it means to be a heavenly-minded Christian.

Love

Paul concluded his discussion of the Christian's wardrobe by reminding us of the most important garment of all—love. The picture here is of a person who has put on every other article of clothing, and then puts on a belt to hold it all in place: "And beyond all these things put on love, which is the perfect bond of unity" (Col. 3:14). Love is the quality that binds all of these other Christian graces together.

Paul emphasized the preeminence of love in 1 Corinthians 13:

If I speak with the tongues of men and of angels, but do not have love, I have become a noisy gong or a clanging cymbal. And if I have the gift of prophecy, and know all mysteries and all knowledge; and if I have all faith, so as to remove mountains, but do not have love, I am nothing. And if I give all my possessions to feed the poor, and if I deliver my body to be burned, but do not have love, it profits me nothing. . . . But now abide faith, hope, love, these three; but the greatest of these is love. (1 Cor. 13:1–3, 13)

The word translated "love" is the well-known Greek word *agape*. It is distinguished from sexual love (*eros*) or brotherly love (*philia*). The word *agape* was rare in Greek literature, but prominent in the New Testament. *Agape* love is a self-sacrificing love that is more concerned with giving than receiving. This love is best exemplified by God who loved the world so much that He gave His Son. Paul says that it is out of this basic attitude toward others that compassion, kindness, humility, gentleness, and patience flow. And it is this quality that best measures the degree of our heavenly-mindedness.

Hopefully you are in the habit of checking your car's engine oil on a regular basis. Oil is the lubricant that makes the engine run smoothly. Without it, your engine will quickly burn up. It would be very difficult to actually look into the crankcase and see how much oil is present in your engine. Instead, the manufacturer has provided a dipstick. All you must do is pull that dipstick out, and you can easily see how much oil is in the engine.

In the same way, there is a readily visible measurement of our commitment to God. It is our love for other people. If our affections and thoughts are set "on things above," then our lives are going to be characterized by compassion, kindness, humility, gentleness, patience, and love toward others.

✳

ACTION STEPS

1. Identify the specific needs you see in the following people:

Your spouse: _____

Your children: _____

Your work associates: _____

Your fellow church members: _____

2. What are some specific steps you could take to help meet those needs? _____

_____

_____

3. Using the definition of kindness from this chapter, list specific acts of kindness you could perform this week for the following people:

Your spouse: _____

Your employer/employee: _____

Your pastor: _____

Your neighbor: _____

4. Name the three accomplishments in your life of which you are most proud. Beside each, list a person who was instrumental in helping you achieve that goal:

a. _____

b. _____

c. _____

5. Is there someone who has deeply hurt or offended you? Have you truly forgiven that person? If not, take a moment and ask God to help you release that offense on the basis of His unconditional forgiveness of us.

6. Memorize and meditate on Colossians 3:12–14.

PART THREE

The Steps to Becoming Heavenly-Minded

And let the peace of Christ rule in your hearts, to which indeed you were called in one body; and be thankful. Let the word of Christ richly dwell within you, with all wisdom teaching and admonishing one another with psalms and hymns and spiritual songs, singing with thankfulness in your hearts to God. And whatever you do in word or deed, do all in the name of the Lord Jesus, giving thanks through Him to God the Father.

— COLOSSIANS 3:15–17

SEVEN

The Secret to Lasting Peace

Read the newspaper, watch television news, or even listen to many evangelical preachers, and you will discover plenty of things to worry about. Barry Siegel once wrote a satirical article in the *Los Angeles Times* entitled "World May End with a Splash" that demonstrates the result of allowing worry to rule our thoughts:

> Alarmists, worrying about such matters as nuclear holocaust and pesticide poisoning, may be overlooking much more dire catastrophes. Consider what some scientists predict: If everyone keeps stacking *National Geographics* in garages and attics instead of throwing them away, the magazine's weight will sink the continent 100 feet sometime soon and we will all be inundated by the oceans.
>
> If the number of microscope specimen slides submitted to one St. Louis Hospital laboratory continues to increase at its current rate, that metropolis will be buried under 3 feet of glass by the year 2024. If beachgoers keep returning home

with as much sand clinging to them as they do now, 80% of the country's coastline will disappear in 10 years.

It has also been reported that pickles cause cancer, communism, airline tragedies, auto accidents and crime waves. About 99.9% of cancer victims had eaten pickles some time in their lives. . . . So have 100% of all soldiers, 96.8% of Communist sympathizers and 99.7% of those involved in car and air accidents. Moreover those born in 1839 who ate pickles have suffered 100% mortality rate and rats force-fed 20 pounds of pickles a day for a month ended up with bulging abdomens and loss of appetite.[1]

Whew! There are a lot of things to worry about—unless you are a heavenly-minded Christian. Now please don't misunderstand. Being a follower of Christ does not exempt you from problems. Jesus was up-front with His disciples about the trials they would encounter: "In the world you *will* have tribulation" (John 16:33, NKJV; emphasis mine). Be assured that if you are a Christian, you are going to have problems at your job, in your family, with your finances, in your church, and with your health. You can bank on it! I love the way the apostle Peter said it: "Beloved, do not be surprised at the fiery ordeal among you, which comes upon you for your testing, *as though some strange thing were happening to you*" (1 Pet. 4:12, emphasis mine). Problems are the price we pay for living in this world.

But Jesus didn't stop there. He went on to promise His followers that they could experience victory over life's problems: "But take courage; I have overcome the world" (John 16:33). The last gift that Jesus left His followers was a supernatural peace of mind that would allow them to cope with life's uncertainties: "Peace I leave with you; My peace I give to you; not as the world gives, do I give to you. Let not your heart be troubled, nor let it be fearful" (John 14:27). But notice something interesting in Jesus' words. Peace is not only a *gift*, it is a *command*. Jesus says, "I am giving you peace, and I want you to apply that peace to your life."

Paul made a similar point in Colossians 3:15. The only way to experience the supernatural gift of peace is to make a conscious decision to allow peace, instead of fear, to rule in your heart: "And *let* the peace of Christ rule in your hearts, to which indeed you were called in one body" (emphasis mine). Allowing the peace of Christ to reign in your heart is the first step to becoming a heavenly-minded Christian. To see how this verse fits in Paul's flow of thought, let's review what we have already seen in Colossians 3.

In Colossians 3:1–4, Paul urged us to become heavenly-minded Christians. If we are believers in Christ, we should have as our primary desire becoming like Jesus Christ. That means conforming our attitudes, our affections, and our actions to the image of Christ. To be heavenly-minded means to love what Jesus loves, to think as Jesus thinks, and to behave as Jesus would behave in our everyday lives.

Second, in Colossians 3:5–12 Paul discussed the *results* of being heavenly-minded. If indeed this transformation is taking place in our affections, attitudes, and actions, there are going to be some noticeable differences in our lives. We will put to death certain behaviors: immorality, impurity, passion, evil desire, and greed (v. 5). We will also lay aside certain behaviors: anger, wrath, malice, slander, abusive speech, and lying (vv. 8–9). The heavenly-minded Christian not only takes off negative behavior, but he clothes himself with positive behavior. His life will be marked by compassion, kindness, humility, gentleness, patience, and love (vv. 12–15).

But how does such a transformation take place? How can I eliminate these negative qualities and develop these Christlike qualities in my life? In this third section of

Colossians 3 (vv. 15–17), Paul is going to mention four steps to becoming a heavenly-minded person:

1. Allow Christ's peace to rule in your heart.

2. Meditate on God's Word.

3. Minister to others.

4. Express gratitude to God.

We are now going to look at some practical ways to allow Christ's peace to rule in your heart.

Understanding the Peace of Christ

What does Paul mean by allowing "the peace of Christ to rule in your hearts"? Obviously, there are two important concepts to understand here. The first is the peace of Christ. The word peace means "absence of turmoil or hostility." If you examine the list of negative actions that a heavenly-minded Christian is to either put to death or lay aside (see vv. 5–9), you will notice one common denominator—turmoil.

In contrast to a heavenly-minded person, the earthly-minded person's life is characterized by turmoil—turmoil within himself and turmoil in relationships with others. The first list of negative actions, found in verse 5, is the result of inner turmoil. It pictures a person who is not at peace with himself. He has a vacuum in his life that he tries to fill with immorality, impurity, or greed.

Solomon was a living illustration of such a person. The Book of Ecclesiastes is a journal of Solomon's attempt to find purpose in life. Solomon's journey led him along the same trail that many people follow today in pursuit of lasting joy. He tried to find satisfaction through sex, narcotics, wealth, wisdom, and work. Yet at the end of his search, he concluded that life apart from God is "meaningless, a chasing after the wind" (Eccl. 1:14, NIV). Even though Solomon reigned over a thriving nation, accumulated vast wealth, enjoyed the company of a thousand women, and was considered the world's wisest man, he spent the majority of his life in personal turmoil.

The second list of negative actions, found in verses 8–9, is an outgrowth of inner turmoil. If a person is not at peace with himself, he cannot be at peace with others. His relationships will be characterized by anger, wrath, malice, slander, abusive speech, and lying.

Paul was saying in verse 15 that there is only one way to be at peace with yourself and others, and that is by allowing the peace of Christ to rule in your life. The command to "let the peace of Christ rule in your hearts" means to allow the same peace to permeate your life that characterized the life of Christ.

Christ's inner peace overflowed into His relationships with others. How did Christ respond to the abuse and false accusations of others? Not with the anger, malice, and abusive speech Paul described in Colossians 3:8. Instead, Christ's inner peace controlled His reactions to His mistreatment by others. "While being reviled, He did not revile in return; while suffering, He uttered no threats, but kept entrusting Himself to Him who judges righteously" (1 Pet. 2:23).

At the foundation of Jesus' belief system was the assurance that God was controlling every part of His life. And that assurance allowed Him to experience peace—the absence of turmoil—in His inner life and in His relationship with others.

Let's stop here for a moment and take a pop quiz. How would you respond to the news that . . .

Your retirement account had been wiped out through a bad investment?

Your home had been lost in a fire?
You had been fired because of a false allegation
by a fellow employee?
Your spouse had been killed in an automobile accident?

Obviously, no one would welcome such news. But could you honestly say that you would experience the same peace that Christ enjoyed when faced with adverse circumstances? The first step to becoming a heavenly-minded Christian is to allow the same peace that governed Christ's life to govern your life, which leads to the second concept in this verse: "to rule in your hearts."

The word *rule* is an athletic term that means "to umpire." The idea is that whenever conflicts arises in your life—whether within yourself or with other people—you have a choice to make. You can respond with fear or anger, or you can allow the peace of Christ to have the final say in your life.

At a meeting of an umpire's convention, some of the participants gathered together for a late-night bull session. The question arose as to how they made difficult calls. One umpire said, "I call them the way I see them." The second umpire said, "I call them the way they are." The third umpire, shaking his head, said, "They ain't nothing until I call them!"

Life's circumstances are like that. We can't always control what situations will be thrown at us; but we can control our response to those circumstances. Adversities are really nothing until we "call them." When problems come into our lives, Paul is urging us to allow Christ's peace to have the final word.

"Great, Robert, but how do I do that? How can I allow peace to rule in my heart?" I believe there are four important steps that will allow you to consistently experience the peace of Christ in every area of your life:

Four Steps to Peace

Experience Peace with God

Imagine a person trying to umpire a baseball game or referee a football game without being in the stadium. It would be impossible. In the same way, it is impossible to allow Christ's peace to rule your life if He is not present *in* your life. How does a person consistently choose contentment over greed, compassion over indifference, kindness over harshness, humility over conceit, gentleness over anger, patience over vengeance, and love over hate? By allowing the "peace of Christ to rule" in one's heart. But before you can make those behavior choices we have talked about in the last few chapters, Christ must first be *in* your heart.

Reading between the lines of Colossians 3, you get the idea that there were conflicts in the church—not as severe as in Corinth, but nevertheless dangerous if left unresolved. However, before the Colossians could allow the peace of Christ to rule in their congregation, He had to first rule in the hearts of the individual members. In his excellent commentary on Colossians, Richard Melick notes that the word rule in this verse is in the plural form: "Since the term is plural and distributive, the heart of each member is implied. The individual hearts had to be at peace for the congregation to be at peace."[2] In other words, the Colossians would never experience the peace of God until they were at peace *with* God.

I have often seen this truth played out in church business meetings. I think of one deacon in a former church whose life was characterized by turmoil. His company had just been sold, and he was fearful of losing his job. His teenage children were running wild. His wife was domineering and told him every move to make. Guess where he chose to take out all of his frustrations? You guessed correctly—in the church. Every month at our deacons' meeting he poured out one complaint after another. Over a period of time he was able to gather a few other deacons who were similarly frustrated, and they tried (unsuccessfully) to split the church. Paul was reminding the Colossians that before they could experience peace with one another in the church, they must first experience peace with God.

How can you experience peace with God? Fortunately, the Bible clearly answers that question. Romans 5:1 says, "Therefore having been justified by faith, we have peace with God through our Lord Jesus Christ." When we acknowledge our sin to God and place our trust in Christ's sacrificial death to pay for our sin, the dividing wall between God and us is abolished and we have peace with God.

Colossians 3 urges us to be like Jesus Christ in every area of our lives. But it is impossible to be like Jesus until He is first ruling in your heart. Do you desire peace within yourself? Are you tired of the emptiness in your life that causes you to constantly chase after money, immorality, or success? The only way to experience peace within is to have peace with God.

Do you desire peace in your relationships with others—your spouse, your children, your parents, your work associates, your friends? Again, the only way you will experience peace with others is to be at peace with God.

Identify Life Areas that Rob You of Peace

Establishing peace with God is the first step to experiencing Christ's peace in your life—but it is not the only step. Unfortunately, Christians still have to deal with worry, even when they are at peace with God. As you look through the Bible, you will find that some of those believers who were closest to Jesus Christ still had difficulty experiencing the peace of God.

Timothy, the pastor at Ephesus, had a problem with worry. Paul had to remind him that "God hath not given us the spirit of fear, but of power, and of love, and of a sound mind" (2 Tim. 1:7, KJV).

The apostles who lived with Jesus for three years still had difficulty gaining victory over worry. Jesus told them, "Do not be anxious for your life, as to what you shall eat, or what you shall drink; nor for your body, as to what you shall put on. Is not life more than food, and the body than clothing"? (Matt. 6:25).

The church at Philippi was a model church in many ways, yet the members had difficulty with anxiety. And so Paul commanded them: "Be anxious for nothing, but in everything by prayer and supplication with thanksgiving let your requests be made known to God" (Phil. 4:6).

I believe that worry is one of Satan's favorite tools to use against a Christian. I remember reading a story about the day the devil decided to go out of business. He announced a sale at which he would dispose of his favorite tools from over the years. The night of the sale, all of Satan's favorite tools were displayed—sexual temptation, greed, hate, and jealousy. Each one had a price attached to it. Off to the side lay a small, wedge-shaped tool which was more worn than the rest. Someone asked Satan why this tool was priced so high. "Oh, that tool is worry." "Why is it priced so much higher than the other tools?" the prospective buyer asked. "Because," the devil explained, "with that tool I can pry into a person's mind when I couldn't get near him with the other tools. Once worry gets inside, then I can allow all the other tools to do their work."[3]

The word worry comes from an Old English word which means "to strangle." And that is what worry does—it strangles us spiritually, emotionally, and even physically. The late Corrie ten Boom once observed, "Worry doesn't empty tomorrow of its sorrow; it empties today of its strength."[4]

You will never become a heavenly-minded Christian as long as you are bogged down with worry. That is why in Colossians 3:15 Paul said that the first step in becoming heavenly-minded is to allow Christ's peace, instead of Satan's fears, to rule our lives. To successfully conquer anxiety, we must identify those areas that rob us of peace. Let me suggest several life areas that can be a source of anxiety:

Finances: "What is going to happen to our economy?" "Will my company still be in business ten years from now?" "How can I ever hope to save enough money for my children's education and my own retirement with my income?" "How can I afford to take care of my aging parents and my own family at the same time?"

Relationships: "I am still bitter about the way _____ wronged me." "I know I hurt _____, but I don't know what to do."

Unconfessed sin: "I'm afraid God is getting ready to punish me because of this sin." "I'm scared someone is going to find out about my relationship with _____."

Neglected responsibilities: "I know I need to start this project, but I don't know where to begin." "I need to schedule an appointment with the doctor, but I am afraid of what he will discover."

Finances may be no problem for you. But you may have several relationships that are causing turmoil in your life. Maybe you have no trouble starting and completing tasks you need to perform, but there is unconfessed sin in your life that is stealing your peace of mind. To allow the peace of Christ to have the final say in your life, you must first identify those things that are robbing you of peace.

Remove Unnecessary Anxiety from Your Life

In his book *The Applause of Heaven,* Max Lucado tells an interesting story about a professional bandit named Black Bart:

> During his reign of terror between 1875 and 1883, he is credited with stealing the bags and the breath away from twenty-nine different stagecoach crews. And he did it all without firing a shot. His weapon was his reputation. His ammunition was intimidation. A hood hid his face. No victim ever saw him. No artist ever sketched his features. No sheriff could ever track his trail. He never fired a shot or took a hostage. He didn't have to. His presence was enough to paralyze. . . .
>
> As it turns out, he wasn't anything to be afraid of, either. When the hood came off, there was nothing to fear. When the authorities finally tracked down the thief, they didn't find a blood thirsty bandit from Death Valley; they found a mild-mannered druggist from Decatur, Illinois. The man the papers pictured storming through the mountains on horseback was, in reality, so afraid of horses he rode to and from his robberies in a buggy. He was Charles E. Boles—the bandit who never once fired a shot, because he never once loaded his gun.[5]

I have a sneaking suspicion that if you were to "unhood" those things causing you the most turmoil in your life you would discover they are not nearly the formidable adversaries you thought them to be. For example:

➤ Balancing your checkbook might reveal you're not in nearly as bad shape as you feared.

➤ Going to the dentist after eleven years might reveal that your teeth are in better shape than you thought.

➤ Meeting for a cup of coffee with that person you have been avoiding for months might reveal that the gulf between you is not as wide as you imagined.

➤ Talking with your heavenly Father might reveal that He is closer than you could have ever hoped.

Satan delights in attacking God's children with unrealistic fears. Perhaps that is why Jesus referred to him as "a liar, and the father of lies" (John 8:44). Instead of running from your fears, confront them. This is not some positive thinking psychobabble. It is a thoroughly biblical way to allow the peace of Christ to have the final say in your life.

A number of years ago, I was returning from a mission trip to Mexico City. While sitting in the Mexico City airport one morning, I was suddenly overwhelmed by one specific fear. Sensing that Satan was trying to pry his way into my mind, I decided to "unhood" my fear. I pulled my legal pad out of my briefcase and wrote across the top of the page the specific fear I was experiencing. Then I divided the page into three columns. The first column was labeled "Reasons This Probably Won't Happen." Under that heading I listed five reasons this fear probably was unfounded. I labeled the second column "What I Would Do If This Happens." I then listed about six action steps to take if my fear was realized. I came to the conclusion that I could survive this disaster if it occurred. The final column on my pad was labeled "Benefits of This Event." I actually listed some positive consequences of such a misfortune taking place. The result? My fear departed as quickly as it had come. I still have the piece of paper in my file as a reminder of the value of confronting fear.[6]

Maintain Consistent Communication with God

If you want to read a firsthand account of someone who allowed the peace of Christ to rule in his heart in spite of adversity, read Paul's letter to the Philippians. The apostle was imprisoned, possibly facing death. Yet he refused to allow his adverse circumstances to rob him of his joy.

What was Paul's secret for experiencing the peace of Christ? He gave two powerful antidotes to fear and turmoil. The first is *prayer.* "Be anxious for nothing, but in everything by prayer and supplication with thanksgiving let your requests be made known to God. And the peace of God, which surpasses all comprehension, shall guard your hearts and your minds in Christ Jesus (Phil. 4:6–7). Paul compared prayer to a Roman guard who marches around a fortress. Just as that guard protects the fortress, prayer protects our minds against the attacks of Satan.

Paul named a second powerful deterrent to fear: *meditation on God's Word.* "Finally, brethren, whatever is true, whatever is honorable, whatever is right, whatever is pure, whatever is lovely, whatever is of good repute, if there is any excellence and if anything worthy of praise, let your mind dwell on these things . . . and the God of peace shall be with you" (Phil. 4:8–9). What is it that is "true, honorable, right, pure, and lovely"? I believe Paul is primarily referring to God's Word. (See Ps. 19:7–10 which uses many of these descriptions for the Word of God.) There is something about meditating on God's Word that allows peace to rule in our lives. Really, that is not hard to understand. In many ways the Bible is simply a record of God's past faithfulness to His people. Just as God has been faithful to those who have obeyed Him in the past, He promises to do the same for us today. We will discuss meditating on God's Word more in the next chapter.

Prayer and meditating on Scripture freed Paul to be a heavenly-minded Christian, in spite of his circumstances. He was not consumed by his circumstances, but by what God was doing *through* his circumstances. God promises that that same peace of mind is available to you, when you choose to allow Christ's peace to rule in your heart.[7]

✳

Action Steps

1. Briefly describe your conversion experience that resulted in peace with God. _____

_____

_____

2. Identify those things which are robbing you of peace in your life:

Financial concerns: _____

_____

Unconfessed sins: _____

_____

Neglected responsibilities: _____

_____

3. List three specific steps you could take to confront some of the above concerns. _____

_____

_____

_____

4. Relate an experience in which you enjoyed the supernatural peace of God in the middle of adverse circumstances. _____

_____

_____

_____

5. Try the same exercise the author used in the Mexico City airport. List your greatest fear at the top of a piece of paper. Then divide it into three headings: "Why This Probably Won't Happen," "What I Would Do If This Happened," and "Benefits of This Happening."

6. Memorize Colossians 3:15 and Philippians 4:6–9.

E I G H T

Bright Lights and
Night Lights

Dr. E. M. Blaiklock, professor of classics at Auckland University in New Zealand, has said, "Of all the centuries, the twentieth is most like to the first. Once again, Christians are a small minority in the midst of a despairing and pagan world, and they are confronted on every side with violence, hostility, ignorance, widespread immorality, and existential despair. They are thus thrust back into the very climate of the first century."[1]

Some Christians in Colossae were being swept away by the heresy, immorality, and persecution of their day. Against this backdrop, Paul wrote to the Colossians urging them to remain faithful. Paul said that the only way to survive in such a hostile environment is to stay focused "on the things above." Colossians 3 is about helping a person develop and maintain a heavenly mind-set while residing in a corrupt world.

Beginning in verse 15, Paul listed four steps to becoming a heavenly-minded Christian. In the last chapter we dealt with the first: "Let the peace of Christ rule in your hearts." The second step to becoming heavenly-minded is found in verse 16: "Let the word of Christ richly dwell within you." Commentators differ on what is meant by the phrase "the word of Christ." Some translate the phrase as "the words spoken by Christ." Others believe it means "the words spoken about Christ." I believe both ideas apply.

Paul is urging the Colossians to meditate on the Word of God, which contains both the words spoken by Christ and the words spoken about Christ. Why? The Word of Christ is like a bright light in a dark, corrupt world.

BENEFITS OF THE WORD OF GOD

Throughout the Scripture, God's Word is referred to as a light that gives direction in the darkness:

Thy word is a lamp to my feet, and a light to my path. (Ps. 119:105)

That you may prove yourselves to be blameless and innocent, children of God above reproach in the midst of a crooked and perverse generation, among whom you appear as lights in the world, holding fast the word of life. (Phil. 2:15–16)

And so we have the prophetic word made more sure, to which you do well to pay attention as to a lamp shining in a dark place, until the day dawns and the morning star arises in your hearts. (2 Pet. 1:19)

Maybe you have used a night-light before. As a child, you may have been comforted by the soft glow of the light in the middle of the night. As an adult, you may have found such a light helpful in finding your way to the bathroom or the kitchen in the middle of the darkness. Obviously, you only need a night-light at night. It is not needed in the day when everything is illuminated. God's Word is like such a light. It provides illumination during this time when we live in a dark world. But when "the day dawns"—when Christ returns—He will dispel the darkness.

The second key to becoming like Jesus is to allow the words of Christ to be implanted in your life in order to give you direction. Before we look at some practical ways to allow the Word of God to become a part of your life, let me suggest three positive benefits of the Word of God:

Spiritual Growth

God's plan for every Christian is that she or he grow in the faith. That means that from the moment a person becomes a Christian, God begins to transform that person into the image of Christ. Colossians 2:6–7 explains God's "building program" for Christians more clearly: "As you therefore have received Christ Jesus the Lord, so walk in Him, having been firmly rooted and now being built up in Him and established in your faith, just as you were instructed, and overflowing with gratitude."

To illustrate his point, Paul used two examples. The phrase "having been firmly rooted" refers to a seed that has been placed in good soil. Hopefully the plant will soon begin to grow. We recently planted some small bushes in front of our home. What was our goal in planting them? Obviously, we want them to grow. If they are the same size next year as they are now, something is terribly wrong. If those bushes are alive, they are going to receive nourishment from the soil and grow. In the same way, if you are really in Christ, there should be growth in your life. You will not be the same person you were a year ago, five years ago, or ten years ago.

The phrase "built up in him and established in our faith" alludes to a building. To construct a strong building you first lay a proper foundation, and then you build on that foundation. It is ludicrous to lay a foundation and then not build anything on it.

When I was growing up in Dallas, the Fairmont Hotel was being built right across the street from our church. For months we would watch the progress of that project on our way to worship several times a week. First, they dug a giant hole. Then, they laid the foundation. Next, they erected the steel beams. Then, without warning, the work ceased. For weeks that lapsed into months, that shell of a structure just stood there. Why? The investors had run out of money. The skeleton of the building began to rust and decay. It was an eyesore and an embarrassment to the city.

It is the same with a Christian who does not grow in the faith. When you became a Christian, Jesus Christ (the Cornerstone) was placed in your life. But that was just the beginning. God wants to construct your life to be an exact replica of His Son. The Word of God represents the tools and materials He will use to complete His project.

Weapon Against Sin

We have spent several chapters explaining that a heavenly-minded person is one who has "executed" immorality, impurity, passion, evil desire, and greed. He has also "laid aside" anger, wrath, malice, slander, abusive speech, and lying. For most people that is easier said than done. How can a person gain victory over these sins?

In Ephesians 6:10–17, Paul likened our struggle to become like Christ to a furious battle. Fortunately, God has provided us with all the equipment we need to be successful in such a war. Of the different pieces of armor that Paul mentioned, only one is an offensive weapon—"the sword of the Spirit, which is the word of God" (v. 17). The word Paul used to describe the sword is *machaira*. The *machaira* was not a long sword that the soldier would flail haphazardly, hoping to strike a target. Instead, the word refers to a dagger, six to eighteen inches long, that was used in hand-to-hand combat. The soldier had to be able to use the dagger skillfully to be successful.

It is the same in our use of the Word of God. Our success in defeating Satan's attacks depends upon our ability to use the Word of God skillfully—and that requires constant study. Jesus demonstrated this principle when He was tempted by Satan in the wilderness (see Matt. 4). Three different times Satan tempted the Lord, and each time Jesus repelled those temptations by quoting Scripture.

I have always thought it is interesting that Jesus quoted from the Book of Deuteronomy in each of those instances. Would you be able to use the Book of Deuteronomy skillfully to fight off the attacks of Satan? Frankly, many of us would have a difficult time even *finding* the Book of Deuteronomy! If the Son of God was dependent on an intimate acquaintance with God's Word to defeat temptation, how much more vital is it that we know God's Word? If we are heavenly-minded, we are going to place the same premium on a knowledge of God's Word that Jesus did.

Success in Ministry

As we will see in the next chapter, all Christians are called to be ministers. The apostle Paul compared our ministry to that of an ambassador in 2 Corinthians 5:20: "We are ambassadors for Christ." What is the job description of an ambassador? In Paul's day, the ambassador represented the king or emperor in a foreign country. Inherent in that responsibility was an intimate knowledge of the king's policy and desires. It would be a pretty sorry ambassador who, when questioned about his monarch's thoughts about a certain subject, answered, "I really don't know what he thinks. But this is what *I* think. . . ." Such an ambassador would probably be called home soon!

Every Christian is a representative of the King of kings. If we are to be successful in representing God, we must be intimately acquainted with God's thoughts and desires. When we try to minister to people who are suffering because of depression, marital difficulties, financial bondage, or a myriad of other problems, they need to know what God says, instead of Oprah, Phil, or Geraldo. And the Bible contains that vital information.

One reason you may lack the motivation to study God's Word could be that you are not involved in spiritual service. In Joshua 1:8, God promised Joshua that if he meditated on God's Word constantly, God would give him success: "This book of the law shall not depart from your mouth, but you shall meditate on it day and night, so that you may be careful to do according to all that is written in it; for then you will make your way prosperous, and then you will have success."

Some people rip this verse out of context, supposing that "success" refers to material prosperity. They believe that applying the principles of Scripture will translate into a bigger bank account, a larger home, or a finer automobile. Sometimes that is the case. But it is clear from the context of the passage that the kind of success God had in mind is success in the *spiritual* work for which He had commissioned Joshua. Joshua would be victorious in leading the Israelites into the promised land if he were careful to obey God's instruction. Likewise, God promises us success in the assignments He has given us to fulfill if we allow His Word to guide our steps.

Now that we have seen how Scripture helps us to maintain a heavenly mind-set, let's look at some practical ways to plant the Word of God into your life. Recently, I was presenting this information at the Navigator's Conference Center in Glen Eyrie, Colorado. For years the Navigators have used a diagram of a hand to demonstrate how to incorporate God's Word into your life. Each finger would be labeled with one of these steps. The idea is that "to get a grip" on God's Word, you need all five of these principles. Allow me to expand on those principles.

PLANTING THE WORD OF GOD IN YOUR LIFE

Principle #1: Listen to the Word

Romans 10:17 says that "faith comes from hearing, and hearing by the word of Christ." Listening to sermons in church, to Christian radio/television programs, or to cassette tapes represents the most passive method of receiving spiritual food—and probably the least effective. We are told by learning experts that a person retains only about 10 percent of what he hears. Nevertheless, as one person said, we need a "regular intake through the eargate!"

For the last several years I have been using a machine that simulates cross-country skiing. Words cannot describe how much I loathe spending time on that machine. Recently, however, I decided to redeem those twenty minutes by listening to sermon tapes while exercising. I have found that beginning each day by listening to God's Word has helped me develop a heavenly mind-set that continues the rest of the day. Not only that, but I actually look forward to my exercise time. Okay—I'm exaggerating! At least, I don't dread it as much.

Time spent in driving, exercising, or performing some mundane tasks can be redeemed by listening to a Christian radio program or some helpful cassette tapes.

Principle #2: Read the Word

It is much more effective to see God's Word, rather than merely hear it. The psalmist prayed, "Open my eyes, that I may behold wonderful things from Thy law" (Ps. 119:18).

God chose to reveal Himself through the words of Scripture. Thus, reading the Bible is essential to having the word of Christ implanted in your life.

We all know we should read our Bibles more. As a pastor, I often hear these excuses for not reading the Bible.

Excuse #1: "I don't feel like reading the Bible." All of us can sympathize with that feeling from time to time—even pastors! Not long ago, I saw a man being interviewed on television. This gentleman was protesting U.S. foreign policy by starving himself to death. He had gone without food for several weeks and looked like he was on death's doorstep. One member of the studio audience commented, "You must feel awful!" "No," the protester said, "I feel just fine." A doctor who was on the panel later explained that in the final stages of starvation a person is unaware that he is hungry; thus, he has no motivation to eat. And that is the most critical stage in the process of starvation—the stage that is followed by death.

I've noticed that when I least feel like reading the Bible is usually when I need it the most. I have found that if I will just begin to read God's Word, I will soon realize how hungry I really am!

Excuse #2: "I don't have time to read the Bible." We make time for the things that are important to us. The fact is that more than one-half the books in the New Testament can be read in thirty minutes or less. Yet Americans spend an average of twenty hours a week watching television. Someone has said that if we spent half the time reading the Bible that we spend in front of the tube, we would be a land of spiritual giants! Let me give you a challenge. Why not set a goal of spending thirty minutes in God's Word for every hour you spend watching television or reading the paper?

Excuse #3: "I don't understand what I read." Purchase a translation of the Bible that you *can* understand. If the *King*

James Version doesn't make sense to you, get a translation that does! There are many fine translations of the Bible available, including the *New American Standard Version* (the translation most used in this book) and the *New International Version*.

By the way, make sure that your children have an understandable version of the Bible as well. It is a shame to give kids the idea that the Bible is a book that cannot be understood.

Whether you are a child or an adult, it only makes sense to read from a version of the Bible that you can easily understand.

Excuse #4: "I forget what I read." I once heard a pastor explain his Bible reading program. Instead of trying to read through the Bible in a year, he selects a book of the New Testament and reads through that book every day for the entire month (remember, most of the books of the New Testament can be read in less than thirty minutes). He says that by the end of the month, he has a firm grasp on the contents of the book, since he has read it so frequently. He takes longer books of the New Testament (like Matthew) and breaks them into thirds—taking three months to read those books thirty times. The result is that in about three years, he will have read the entire New Testament thirty times. I tried this method recently and am amazed at how much of the content of each book I remember.

Certainly reading the same material several times can help you retain the material better. But I have also discovered that one reason people don't retain more is that they try to read *too much* of the Bible at one sitting.

Now I know I risk being labeled a heretic by saying this, but you may want to consider throwing away your "Read the Bible Through in a Year" schedules. If they work for you, fine. But many people do not always have the same time to devote to Bible study each day. Yet, when they feel chained to these schedules, they race through their assigned chapters with little comprehension of what they are reading.

I have often wondered why people feel they must read through the Bible in a year, when the Bible took over sixteen hundred years to complete! If you have difficulty retaining what you read in the Bible, try reading smaller portions.

Principle #3: Study the Word

There is a basic difference between an explorer and a tourist. The tourist travels quickly, only stopping to observe highly noticeable points of interest. The explorer, on the other hand, takes his time to search out all that he can find. Too many of us read the Bible like a tourist; then we complain that our devotional times are fruitless. It is necessary that we take time to stop and explore the rich truths of God's Word.

When you read the Bible, there will be some passages that pique your curiosity or that you may not understand. Mark those passages for further study. Every serious student of God's Word should have in addition to the Bible: a concordance, a Bible dictionary, and some commentaries to help dig out the deeper truths of Scripture.

Several years ago, I was at the Billy Graham Center for Evangelism in Wheaton, Illinois. While there, I noticed a Bible that had been given to Albert Einstein. I was particularly interested in the note on the flyleaf of that Bible. It read, "Straws on the surface flow; he who would search for pearls must dive below." The person was reminding Einstein that even a person with his great intellect could not uncover the truths of God's Word without effort. It takes diligent study, coupled with the leading of the Holy Spirit, to truly understand God's Word.

Many good books have been written about how to study the Bible. One of the best is *Living by the Book*, by Howard and William Hendricks. In my book *Guilt-Free Living*, I devote a chapter to the subject of "Guilt-Free Bible Study." I note that whenever you read a portion of the Bible—whether it be a verse, a paragraph, a chapter, or an entire book—there are certain things you should observe: content (what is said) and style (how it is said).

Imagine that a friend asks you about a movie you have seen. How would you describe the movie to him? You would probably try to summarize the content of the movie: "The movie is about a factory owner who saves the lives of eleven hundred Jews during World War II in Poland." Notice that you have used the basic questions "who" (a factory owner), "what" (saves the lives of eleven hundred Jews), "when" (during World War II), and "where" (in Poland) to summarize the content of the movie. Whenever you read the Bible, you can use those same questions to summarize the content of the passage you are studying.

For example, read Ephesians 2:4–6 and then use the above questions (who, what, when, and where) to summarize the passage: "But God, being rich in mercy, because of His great love with which He loved us, even when we were dead in our transgressions, made us alive together with Christ (by grace you have been saved), and raised us up with Him, and seated us with Him in the heavenly places, in Christ Jesus."

Those simple questions reveal profound truths. God (who) raised us up and seated us with Him (what) when we were still dead in our transgressions (when) in the heavenly places (where). What an amazing thought! God saved us, not because we deserved to be saved, but because He loved us. He set the plan of redemption into action while we were still dead in our sins. After you read a verse or paragraph of Scripture, close your Bible and see if you can summarize that passage in terms of who, what, when, and where.

Sometimes *how* something is said is just as important as *what* is being said. The author may use repetition, contrasts, cause-effect relationships, and questions and answers to highlight his message. Notice how many literary devices the psalmist used in Psalm 1 to describe the benefits of memorizing, meditating on, and applying God's Word:

> *How blessed is the man*
> *who does not walk in the counsel of the wicked,*
> *Nor stand in the path of sinners,*
> *Nor sit in the seat of scoffers!*
> *But his delight is in the law of the Lord,*
> *And in His law he meditates day and night,*
> *And he will be like a tree*
> *firmly planted by streams of water,*
> *Which yields its fruit in its season,*
> *And its leaf does not wither;*
> *And in whatever he does, he prospers.*
>
> *The wicked are not so.*
> *But they are like chaff which the wind drives away.*
> *Therefore the wicked will not stand in the judgment,*
> *Nor sinners in the assembly of the righteous.*
> *For the Lord knows the way of the righteous,*
> *But the way of the wicked will perish.*

The psalmist used contrasts to show the difference between the actions of the righteous and the unrighteous. The unrighteous person allows his attitudes to be shaped by ungodly people. However, the righteous person allows his attitudes to be shaped by the Word of God. The righteous person will prosper in whatever he does; the wicked person shall be blown away like worthless chaff.

Notice also how the writer used cause-effect relation-ships in this passage. Meditating on God's Word (the cause) produces success (effect). Associating with ungodly people (cause) brings judgment (effect).

Another literary device the psalmist used effectively is comparison. The person who meditates on God's Word is like a fruitful tree. The ungodly person is like worthless chaff.

As you study the Bible, be aware of these different tools the writers used to emphasize their point. Paying attention to these literary devices will help the Bible come alive to you.

Principle #4: Memorize the Word

To become a heavenly-minded Christian, Paul says that we must allow the Word of God to dwell *in* us—and that means memorizing Scripture. You may be breaking out in a cold sweat at this point thinking, "I can't even remember where I put my car keys last night; how can I remember a passage of Scripture?" Suppose I were to tell you that I would give you $10,000 if you could memorize Colossians 3 in a week. I suspect you would probably accept the challenge. I also imagine that within a week I would hear you recite the passage perfectly. Therefore, let's be honest. The problem you probably have with Scripture memory is not *ability* but *motivation.*

Memorizing God's Word is like putting cash in the bank—it comes in handy on a rainy day! Remember the pastor in the hotel elevator who used the memorized Word of God to keep him from sin? Had the pastor fallen into sin, he could have lost his family, his reputation, and his ministry. Just think how much heartache, embarrassment, and money that one verse of Scripture (Gal. 6:7) saved him!

As you read and study different sections of the Bible, let me suggest that you mark certain key verses that speak to you. Write these verses on index cards and commit them to memory. Or you may want to purchase a Bible memory system like *The Topical Memory System* (published by NavPress) that has preprinted Scripture verses on individual cards you can carry with you.

One word of caution. The purpose of Scripture memory is not to see how many verses you can memorize, but to have God's Word so implanted in your life that in times of temptation or discouragement, or when you need guidance, the memorized Word can come to your rescue.

The other day I was in a meeting and someone made a comment that ticked me off. I was about to make a smart-aleck reply when suddenly Proverbs 29:20 came to mind: "Do you see a man who is hasty in his words? There is more hope for a fool than for him." This verse kept me from saying something I would have deeply regretted. Memorizing God's Word is an important step in shaping our attitudes, actions, and affections to those of Christ.

Principle #5: Meditate on the Word

Many people confuse memorizing Scripture with meditating on Scripture. But there is a significant difference between the two. Unfortunately, I can memorize Scripture without ever meditating on it.

Psalm 1 and Joshua 1:8 promise success to those who meditate on (not simply memorize) God's Word. To meditate on God's Word does not mean to go into some type of hypnotic trance! Instead, the Hebrew word for meditate means "to mutter."

I have a habit of talking to myself. One Sunday a member said, "I drove past you on the freeway and started to honk. But I saw you were having such a deep discussion with yourself, I didn't want to interrupt!"

Actually, that is a good example of meditation. The word describes a person so wrapped up in God's Word that he keeps turning it over in his mind—resulting in his muttering aloud. The psalmist captures the meaning of meditation in Psalm 1: "But they delight in doing everything God wants them to, and day and night are always meditating on his laws and *thinking about ways to follow him more closely*" (Ps. 1:2, TLB, emphasis mine). Did you notice the phrase "thinking of ways to follow him more closely?" That is what meditation is—constantly turning God's Word over in your mind with a view to applying it and asking, "How should the truth of this passage affect my work, my social life, my friendships, my moral life, and my family?"

Many times God's Word will motivate us to make certain changes in our habits, our attitudes, or our relationships. That's what becoming a heavenly-minded Christian is all about.

As we come to the close of this chapter, let's return to Psalm 1 for a moment. What does God promise for the person who allows the word of God to richly dwell within him? "He will be like a tree firmly planted by streams of water, which yields fruit in its season, and its leaf does not wither; and in whatever he does, he prospers" (v. 3). What a picturesque description! In the dry, desert area of Israel, this was an appealing word picture—a large tree that is unmoveable, productive, and consistently bearing fruit.

Do those words describe your life? Is your life marked by stability, or are you easily blown around by life's circumstances? Is your life productive, or are your days filled with meaningless activities? Are you consistent in your faith, or is your spiritual life marked by short bursts of enthusiasm, followed by long droughts of apathy? Both the psalmist and Paul promised stability, productivity, and consistency when you allow God's Word to richly dwell within you.

✳

ACTION STEPS

1. Describe one experience you have had in which God's Word gave you direction in your life. _____

_____

_____

_____

2. What has hindered you from studying the Bible regularly? _____

_____

_____

_____

3. Identify the strongest temptation you are facing in your life right now. What passages in the Bible relate directly to those temptations? _____

_____

_____

_____

4. Commit yourself to reading those passages each day for two weeks. Memorize them if you can.

5. When are some "dead" times you could listen to sermon tapes? _____

_____

What pastors/Bible teachers minister most to you? _____

_____

Contact their offices this week to receive a catalog of available tapes that you might purchase or borrow.

6. Challenge yourself to spend twenty minutes each day reading God's Word. What book of the Bible will you start with? _____

7. Memorize Psalm 1.

NINE

Hooked on Others

Recently, I was in a small group where I heard a woman give this remarkable testimony. The woman had served as a social worker for a state prison system. Being a dedicated Christian, she saw her work as an opportunity to be a witness for Christ to those who needed Him most. One day she entered a small room to meet with a prisoner. They were the only two in the room.

Suddenly, without provocation, the prisoner became violently angry, grabbed the woman, and began choking her. He then proceeded to break every bone in her face. Finally, he took a nail he had been carrying and plunged it into her neck. He was sure he had killed her.

After several days of lying in a coma, the woman says she heard the voice of God speak to her. She recognized the voice as being the same voice that had spoken to her as a small child and called her to faith in Christ. It was the same voice that had spoken to her as a teenager and called her into special ministry. And now, this same voice was calling her back to life. When she awoke, her first thought was that she must return to that prison and share the gospel with that man who had tried to kill her.

Throughout her long recovery she was obsessed with that desire. When she returned to work, prison officials refused to allow her to see her attacker, but she was able to leave a Bible for him and a note saying that she had forgiven him and wanted him to come to faith in Christ. This remarkable Christian had dedicated her life to meeting the spiritual needs of others—including her enemies.

One important step in becoming a heavenly-minded Christian is making our lives ministry-driven rather than self-driven. A person who has truly set his mind on "the things above, where Christ is" will have a desire to pattern his life after that of Jesus Christ. And that means that ministry to others will be a focal point of his life.

In this section we are looking at ways to become a heavenly-minded Christian. The first step is to allow the peace of Christ to rule your life. The second is to allow the word of Christ to permeate your life. The third is the subject of this chapter: ministering to the spiritual needs of others. "Let the word of Christ richly dwell within you with all wisdom teaching and admonishing one another" (Col. 3:16).

One way to become more like Jesus Christ in your actions, affections, and attitudes is to make ministry to others, rather than self-fulfillment, the focus of your life. This is such a simple concept, and yet I am surprised at the number of well-taught Christians who really do not understand (or at least, apply) this truth.

Inject most Christians with a good dose of Sodium Pentothol and ask the question, "What is the purpose of your life?" and they will answer:

To find happiness in life,
To enjoy my family,
To make my mark in my profession,
To earn enough money to retire comfortably.

Now, before you start clucking your tongue and saying "Isn't that just awful?" ask yourself some hard questions.

1. Name one thing you did to benefit someone else this past week for which you received nothing whatsoever. __

_____

_____

2. Imagine that Aunt Bessie dies and leaves you $10,000. What would you *really* do with that money? _____

_____

_____

3. When was the last time you led someone to faith in Jesus Christ? _____

_____

_____

4. What do you plan to do with your time once you reach retirement age? _____

_____

_____

Your answers to these questions will reveal whether your life is ministry-driven or self-driven. This chapter will look at why we should be ministry-driven, how we can become ministry-driven, and the benefits of being a ministry-driven Christian.

THE MANDATE FOR MINISTRY

Unfortunately, many churches do not understand the clearly defined mission God has given to them. One writer summed up the problem well when he observed, "Many a church is like an impressive machine I once read about. It had hundreds of wheels, cogs, gears, pulleys, belts, and lights, which all moved or lit up at the touch of a button. When someone asked, 'What does it do?' the inventor replied, 'Oh, it doesn't do anything—but doesn't it run beautifully?'"[1]

Christ has commanded that the church—that means you and me—do something other than "run beautifully." And that something is explained in Matthew 28:19–20: "Go therefore and make disciples of all the nations, baptizing them in the name of the Father and the Son and the Holy Spirit, teaching them to observe all that I commanded you; and lo, I am with you always, even to the end of the age."

This command represents some of Jesus' final words to His apostles before He ascended into heaven. Last words are important words. I remember well my mother's last words to me before she died of colon cancer, "Robert, be faithful in your ministry." Over the years when I have been faced with temptations and discouragements, God has brought those words to my mind. My mother's final admonition has kept me focused on my life's purpose. In the same way, Jesus' final command to all Christians reminds us that God has left us on earth for one purpose—to make disciples of Christ. If you are going to be a heavenly-minded Christian, you will be channeling your abilities, your time, and your resources toward that one purpose.

But what does it mean to "make disciples"? Obviously, before we can make a disciple, we must know what one looks like! Let's take a moment and define the word *disciple*. *Disciple* comes from a word that means "one who professes to have learned certain principles from another and maintains those principles in his life." In Jesus' day, people would often attach themselves to a respected rabbi so that they might learn from that teacher and imitate his way of life. Using that definition, let me point out two characteristics of a disciple of Christ:

1. A disciple is a Christian. Implicit in disciple-making is evangelism. Jesus said that the first step in the disciple-making process is "baptizing them in the name of the Father and the Son and the Holy Spirit" (Matt. 28:19). I believe that Jesus is referring to conversion here. It is impossible for anyone to be a follower of Christ without first becoming a Christian. Jesus likened the conversion experience to a new birth in John 3. Without such an experience it is impossible to enter into the kingdom of God (see John 3:5). That means that if we are going to take Christ's command to make disciples seriously, we are going to have to learn how to lead people to faith in Christ.

Actually, sharing your faith with another person is not nearly as complicated as some people try to make it. I teach the members of my church how to use a booklet (like *The Four Spiritual Laws* or *Steps to Peace with God)* that explains the gospel clearly and concludes with a prayer of repentance. I encourage them not to worry about memorizing the contents of the booklet—there is nothing wrong with reading it to the person with whom they are sharing.

Many of our members are discovering that they do not have to be Billy Graham to lead someone to faith in Christ. Furthermore, those who share their faith on a regular basis are finding themselves more interested in spiritual matters. My friend Howard Hendricks tells a story that might explain that phenomenon. He said his father, a military man, once told him: "You can always tell where your troops are by what they're complaining about. If they are complaining about warm beer, you know they are nowhere near the front lines; but, if they are complaining about a lack of ammunition, you know that they are in the heat of battle!"

A person who is regularly leading people to Christ will not be complaining that the music is too loud or that the sanctuary is too cold when he comes to church. Instead, he is going to come to church desperate to receive the "ammunition" he needs for the front lines of ministry. He will find himself more focused "on the things above."

2. A disciple obeys Christ in every area of his life. The very definition of the word *disciple* conveys the idea of obedience: "one who professes to have learned certain principles . . . and maintains those principles in his life." Jesus said that if we are in the disciple-making business we will not only lead people to faith in Christ, but we will also teach people to "observe all that I have commanded you."

If our lives are ministry-driven, we are not only going to be interested in seeing people make an initial decision to trust in Christ, we will also want them to apply His teachings to every area of their lives—their marriages, their jobs, their recreational lives, their finances, their friendships, their physical health, etc.

Whenever I preach about the mandate to minister, I read the minds of my congregation.

"Pastor, that is easy for you to say. You have been to seminary and know the Bible, but I have a difficult time even finding some of the books of the Bible."

"You enjoy talking to large groups of people, but I freeze up anytime I have to speak before a group."

"You get paid to make disciples. But I have a *real* job that keeps me busy sixty hours a week."

Paul was not addressing Colossians 3 to a seminary class or to a pastor's conference. When the apostle wrote about "teaching and admonishing one another," he was writing to church *members*, not church *leaders*. Paul was saying that we can all become involved in the disciple-making business, in spite of our gifts or limitations. How?

THE METHOD OF MINISTRY

Paul used two words to describe how we can lead other people to become disciples of Christ. Both words are related to using the Word of God. One word is positive; the other word is negative. But both are essential to the disciple-making process.

Teaching

First, we are to be *teaching* one another. The idea here is to encourage other people by sharing God's Word with them. Notice the relationship between allowing God's Word to dwell within you and using His Word to minister to others. Paul is saying that a natural by-product of meditating on God's Word day and night will be the desire to share His Word with others. When God's Word is richly dwelling within you, it will become a natural part of your conversation with others.

Some time ago I heard an interview with Iran-Contra figure Oliver North. North said that before he entered the Senate hearing room for the Iran-Contra investigation, a woman broke through the crowd, handing him a card with a note on it. He read it and then set the card in front of the microphone as he began days of intensive investigation. When asked what was written on the card, North replied "the answer to everything." What was on the card? The woman had simply copied Isaiah 40:31: "Those who wait for the Lord will gain new strength; they will mount up with wings like eagles, they will run and not get tired; they will walk and not become weary." Oliver North said that the woman's note of encouragement from the Word of God sustained him through that ordeal.

I believe that is what Paul had in mind when he wrote about using God's Word to teach one another. Whenever we think of teaching, we imagine standing before a Sunday

School class or leading a Bible study. Certainly some people are called to do that. But I do not believe that is the idea Paul had in mind here. Notice that Paul added the words "one another" to this command. The idea here is to meet the needs of those you come in contact with by sharing the life-changing principles from God's Word. For example:

➤ If someone who was contemplating divorce came to you for advice, would you know where to turn in the Bible to give them advice?

➤ What if someone asked you what to do with a rebellious teenager? Would you be able to use God's Word to help them?

➤ What if someone told you that they were interested in becoming a Christian? Would you know what verses to use to lead them to faith in Christ?

It is both amazing and disheartening for me to realize that most of the members of my church have been sitting in Sunday School classes for years, and yet would have to answer no to the above questions. Maybe you are one of those people. Yet I believe that one reason you are reading this book is that you want to change. You want to become more heavenly-minded in your daily life. You don't want to wait until heaven to become like Jesus Christ. You are serious about becoming a disciple-maker. What are some practical ways you can begin to impart the principles of God's Word to others?

1. Over the next two weeks jot down the most common problems that you experience personally or that people mention to you. Limit your list to ten. Your "Top Ten" list might include depression, financial problems, loneliness, marital problems, parenting concerns, stress, or anger.

2. Once you have compiled your list, find appropriate Scripture passages that deal with each of these topics. You

might consider using a loose-leaf notebook with a divider for each topic. I would suggest that you use a topical Bible like *Nave's Topical Bible* to assist you. The difference between a concordance and a topical Bible is that a concordance is arranged by specific words, while a topical Bible is arranged by topics. For example, if you were to look up the word *anger* in a concordance, you would find a list of all the passages in the Bible that actually use the word *anger*. However, a topical Bible would list all of the passages that dealt with the subject of anger, including passages using the words *wrath* or *bitterness*.

3. Once you have compiled your list of verses for each of these topics, read through the Bible passages carefully. In your notebook, write down the principles you find about your subject. For example, for the subject of finances you might note the following principles from your study:

➤ We are to avoid debt whenever possible.
➤ We are to pay our bills on time.
➤ We are to give at least a tithe of our income to the church.
➤ We should save some of our income for future needs.
➤ We should never cosign a loan for someone else.
➤ We should never trust in money to solve our problems.

4. Memorize one (or more) relevant passage of Scripture for each of these topics.

5. Go to your church library or Christian bookstore and find at least three good books that relate to each of these topics. Jot down the information about these books in your notebook to remind you to read these yourself or to recommend to others.

Following these simple steps will produce several benefits in your life. First, you will have a focus in your Bible study that is practical rather than theoretical. Second, you will discover for yourself God's principles of living that hopefully will help you become more like Christ. And third, when you encounter people who have a specific need, you will be able to effectively use God's Word to help them shape their lives in the image of Christ. That is what disciple-making is all about.

Admonishing

Another facet of disciple-making is *admonishing* one another. The word *admonishing* carries the idea of warning other people. What are we to warn people about? Certainly we are to warn people of the danger of dying without Christ. Jesus frequently warned His listeners about the horrors of hell (see Luke 16). But I do not think this is what Paul had in mind here.

Remember, the context here is of Christians ministering to one another. Part of our ministry to fellow believers is not only to encourage them with the Word of God (teaching) but to correct them with the Word of God (admonishing). For example, how would you respond in the following situations?:

➤ A Christian friend tells you he (or she) is going to leave his mate. "I no longer feel fulfilled in the relationship." Your friend is not asking your advice, he is simply stating his intentions. How would you respond?

➤ Your employer professes to be a Christian. However, he orders you to do something that is blatantly dishonest and unethical. What would you say to him?

➤ A member of your church shares his or her dissatisfaction with the pastor. "I do not feel he is God's man for our church any longer." How would you react?

Let's face it, most of us would feel more comfortable remaining mute in any of the above situations. While all of our excuses seem logical (and even biblical), they are easy ways for us to shirk one of our basic responsibilities—admonishing. We are to use God's Word to encourage, as well as rebuke; to edify, as well as to correct. In 2 Timothy 3:16, Paul wrote of the multiple purposes of God's Word: "All Scripture is inspired by God and profitable for teaching, for *reproof*, for *correction*, for training in righteousness; that the man of God may be adequate, equipped for *every good work*" (emphasis mine).

I notice two things in that well-known verse. First, one of the purposes of God's Word is correction. Second, correction (or admonition) is labeled as a "good work." No, correcting another Christian is not pleasant—and it can be extremely risky. Nevertheless, it is an important part of the disciple-making process. James echoed the same thought in his epistle: "Let him know that he who turns a sinner from the error of his way will save his soul from death, and will cover a multitude of sins" (Jas. 5:20).

Just as a surgeon must be trained to effectively use a scalpel, we must skillfully use the Word of God when we use it to cut and correct another Christian. How do you admonish a person in "wisdom"? Let me share several principles I have discovered from God's Word and from experience about admonishing other Christians:

1. Make restoration, not retribution, your goal in admonishing another Christian. In 1 Corinthians 5, Paul addressed the subject of discipline in the church. A member of the Corinthian church was having an affair with his stepmother. What was the church's response? They bragged about the fact that they were not dealing with the problem. I can just hear some of them now: "We are not a judgmental church.

We are all sinners saved by grace. Our responsibility is to accept people just as they are and let God deal with them." Yet Paul condemned them for not handling the matter. He pointed out that refusing to admonish him about his sin was a disservice to both the church *and* the sinner. The church's witness in the community was damaged and the sinner was estranged from God.

Instead, Paul commanded that the church discipline the member and turn him out of the church if he refused to repent. Why such severe treatment? "I have decided to deliver such a one to Satan for the destruction of his flesh, *that his spirit may be saved* in the day of the Lord Jesus" (1 Cor. 5:5, emphasis mine). Paul's purpose in admonishing this man was not retribution, but restoration.

Jesus said the same thing in Matthew 18:15–20. In this passage he gave specific steps for admonishing a fellow believer. Notice what He commanded to be done first: "And if your brother sins, go and reprove him in private; if he listens to you, you have won your brother." The best-case scenario, Jesus said, is that when you warn a fellow Christian of his sin, he responds positively. You have played a part in restoring him to a right relationship to God. That is the goal of admonition.

2. When admonishing another Christian, keep it as private as possible. Imagine someone comes to you and says that she has proof that your Bible study leader is having an affair. What should be your first response?

a. Share your concern with your pastor?

b. Ask two close friends to pray about this matter?

c. Go talk to the Bible study leader?

In Matthew 18:15–20 Jesus taught that "c" is the correct answer. Notice the steps in admonishing a Christian:

a. Go talk to him privately (18:15) If he responds positively, drop the matter. If he doesn't . . .

b. Take one or more Christians with you to confront him (18:16). Again, if he repents of his sin, you have succeeded in your mission. If he still refuses to admit his sin . . .

c. Report it to the church (18:17a). The church needs to be informed about the issue. Why? Not for gossip, but to pray that the individual might be restored. If he still refuses to repent . . .

d. Turn him out of the church (18:17b). This is what happened to the man in Corinth. Remember, the goal in this drastic action is not to punish the individual but to restore him. Hopefully, the action will convince him of the seriousness of his sin and motivate him to repent.

3. Deal with unconfessed sin in your own life before you try to admonish another Christian. Jesus said it this way in Matthew 7:1–5:

> Do not judge lest you be judged. For in the way you judge, you will be judged; and by your standard of measure, it will be measured to you. And why do you look at the speck that is in your brother's eye, but do not notice the log that is in your own eye? Or how can you say to your brother, "let me take the speck out of your eye," and behold, the log is in your own eye? You hypocrite, first take the log out of your own eye, and then you will see clearly to take the speck out of your brother's eye.

Some use the above passage as proof that we are never to judge another Christian. "Do not judge, lest you be judged" they remind us. Yet, the word translated "judge" refers to a condemning type of judgment, rather than a restorative judgment. No, we are not to pronounce a final sentence on anyone. Nor are we to criticize others to elevate ourselves, as the Pharisees did. But Jesus said there is nothing wrong with removing the "speck" from your brother's eye, as long as you remove the log out of your own eye first.

Imagine a surgeon trying to perform an operation while blindfolded! Who would want to be on the operating table for that? Yet that is a perfect picture of what happens when a Christian tries to correct a fellow Christian without first dealing with the sin in his own life. He is not able to "see clearly" to perform spiritual surgery.

I have experienced the same thing in my own ministry. For example, if I've been guilty of gossip, I will go to one of two extremes. I may avoid preaching on the topic since it is a blindspot in my own life. Or, I might deal harshly with other gossipers out of frustration over my own problem with this vice. What I should do is remove the sin from my life. Then I can see clearly to help others.

In this chapter we have seen that a heavenly-minded Christian views life from a ministry perspective. He understands that his major assignment in life is to "make disciples" of Christ. The mission of disciple-making includes evangelism, but it is much more than evangelism. Jesus defined discipleship as teaching people "to observe all things" He commanded. How do we do that? Paul said disciple-making involves using the Word of God to teach and admonish one another.

The Motivation for Ministry

As I bring this chapter to a close, I want us to look at some positive benefits from having a ministry-driven, rather than a self-driven, life.

1. Ministry gives us a purpose for living. I recently read a survey of ninety-year-olds that asked the question, "If you had your life to live over again, what would you do differently?" The top answers were: (1) "Risk more;" (2) "Not take life so seriously;" and (3) "Do more things that would live on after I die." All of us need a purpose greater than ourselves to which to devote ourselves. And devoting ourselves to God's Great Commission is the greatest purpose in the universe.

2. Ministry helps us to view adversity differently. My friend Bobb Biehl says, "Every life exists for one of two purposes: to fill a need or to fill a greed." If the purpose of our life is self, then every adversity is a negative. On the other hand, if our life purpose is ministry to others, we can view adversity as a way to help us achieve that purpose.

Paul could have become discouraged about his circumstances. If his life purpose had been personal peace and prosperity, his imprisonment was a definite detour. But Paul's life purpose was ministry to others. Thus, when he viewed his imprisonment through the lens of that purpose, he saw positive benefits from his imprisonment. First, the guards to whom he was chained were hearing the gospel. Furthermore, other Christians were gaining boldness to proclaim the Word of God because of Paul's example.

What is your life purpose? If your life is self-driven, then the inevitable adversities of life—financial problems, the death of loved ones, illness—are handicaps. But if your life is ministry-driven, all those problems can actually be ministry opportunities in disguise. Remember the woman I wrote about at the beginning of this chapter? Because she had devoted her life to ministry, she was able to turn her negative circumstances into a positive opportunity.

3. Ministry frees me from bitterness. My mother used to have a saying that I carry with me to this day: "Great offenses reveal great needs." When someone hurts me, accuses me, or disappoints me, it is symptomatic of a deeper need they possess. It may be a need for affirmation, forgiveness, or repentance. But unless I am ministry-driven, I will react negatively to that offense rather than view it as an opportunity for ministry.

Certainly the great example of forgiveness in the Old Testament is Joseph. You probably remember the story. Joseph was sold into slavery by his brothers. But through a series of miraculous circumstances, Joseph became Pharaoh's right-hand man, in charge of food distribution. A severe famine in the land caused Joseph's brothers to travel to Egypt to ask for food. Little did they realize that the man to whom they would make their appeal would be their brother. When they came face to face with Joseph, they were terrified. Surely Joseph would have them killed for their offense. But Joseph said to them, "'And as for you, you meant evil against me, but God meant it for good in order to bring about this present result, to preserve many people alive. So therefore, do not be afraid; I will provide for you and your little ones.' So he comforted them and spoke kindly to them" (Gen. 50:20–21).

When I read this passage, I notice several things about Joseph. Joseph never denied that his brothers had hurt him ("You meant it for evil"). But instead of focusing on what his brothers had done, Joseph focused on what God was doing through his brothers ("but God meant it for good in order to bring about this present result to preserve many people alive"). Through the brothers' act of vengeance, Joseph had ended up in Egypt where he was able to provide food for his family. Had Joseph not been in Egypt, there would have been no brothers, no nation of Israel, no Jesus Christ, and ultimately no salvation for the world. Joseph saw the big picture. And that allowed him to minister to his brothers rather than to react against them.

The next time someone hurts you, don't ask, "Why are they doing this to me?" Instead, ask, "What need does this person have that I can meet?" and "What is God trying to do in this situation?" Who knows, He might use you to save an entire nation!

4. *Ministry ensures eternal rewards.* Luke 16: 1–9 contains one of Jesus' most fascinating, and yet perplexing, parables.

It is the story of a financial manager about to lose his job. He is given only a few days to get his affairs in order. Realizing he will soon be out of a job, he needs to figure out how to use the short time he has left in his job to prepare for the future. He comes up with a shrewd, though dishonest, scheme. He will discount all of the accounts receivable owed his master. That way, once the financial manager joins the ranks of the unemployed, these people whom he has assisted will do him a favor.

Contrary to what some have thought, Jesus is not praising the manager for his dishonesty. Instead, Jesus was complimenting him on his foresight. This steward realized that he had a limited time left in his position. Instead of panicking, he used his present opportunities to prepare for the future. Jesus said we should do the same as Christians.

Gary Inrig tells the story about a man who was shipwrecked on an island. He discovered a large tribe of people on the other end of the island. The people treated the man very well. They placed him on a throne and met his every need. He could not understand why they were so hospitable. Then he learned the truth. The tribe had a custom of selecting a man to be king for one year. Then they would transport him to a neighboring island and abandon him.

As he contemplated his future, he began to panic. But then, he devised a shrewd plan. Over the next months he ordered different groups of people to work on the other island. They tilled the land, planted trees, and built a beautiful home. He even sent some of his best friends to live on that deserted island. When the year came to an end and he was dispatched to the island, he had a beautiful home and wonderful friends to welcome him.[2]

A heavenly-minded Christian realizes his time on earth is short. However, instead of panicking, he uses the resources God has given him in this life to prepare for the future. When we channel our time, abilities, and money into fulfilling the Great Commission, we can be sure that there will be people in heaven to greet us when we arrive.

✳

ACTION STEPS

1. As you think about your closest friends, what spiritual or emotional needs do they have? _____

_____

_____

_____

2. As we will see in chapter 11, our most important ministry is in our own home. What spiritual or emotional needs do you see in your spouse? What about in your children? _____

_____

_____

_____

3. Begin to compile the suggested ministry notebook on pages 130–32.

4. List three friends, family members, or acquaintances you believe need to become Christians. _____

_____

_____

_____

5. If given the opportunity, would you know how to lead them to become Christians? If not, purchase a simple evangelistic booklet from your church or local Christian bookstore. Become well-acquainted with the material in the booklet and pray for an opportunity to share the booklet with those whom you have listed.

6. Is there someone whom you need to admonish? Carefully think through what you would say to that person and then pray for the opportunity to confront that individual in a loving way.

7. Memorize Matthew 28:19–20.

T E N

Count Blessings,
Not Sheep

In her wonderful book *The Hiding Place*, Corrie ten Boom tells how she learned to be thankful in every situation. She and her sister Betsy had been moved to Ravensbruck—the most horrible of all the Nazi death camps. When they arrived in the barracks, they found that the sleeping quarters were overcrowded and flea-infested.

Earlier that morning, the two sisters had been reading 1 Thessalonians 5:18: "In everything give thanks; for this is God's will for you in Christ Jesus." Betsy suggested that she and Corrie pause to thank God for everything about their new accommodations—including the fleas. Corrie writes that at first she refused to thank God for the fleas, but her sister persisted. Finally, Corrie relented and thanked God for the fleas in her barracks.

As the months unfolded, Corrie and Betsy were surprised at how easily they were able to conduct Bible studies and prayer meetings without interference from the prison guards. Finally, they learned the reason: the guards would not enter the barracks because of the fleas.

Learning to thank God for everything in our lives—including the "fleas"—is but another step in becoming a heavenly-minded Christian. Remember the second verse of the old song "Count Your Blessings"? "Are you ever burdened with a load of care? Does the cross seem heavy you are called to bear? Count your many blessings every doubt will fly, and you will be singing as the days go by." The words may seem a little corny today; but they remind us of an important truth: Expressing gratitude to God has a way of transporting our thoughts from this world to the heavenly world. Regularly thanking God for everything in our lives helps us to "set our minds on the things above."

Paul drew the same parallel between gratitude and developing a heavenly mind-set in Colossians 3:15–17. Here, he explained how to become heavenly-minded:

1. Let the peace of Christ rule in your heart.

2. Let the word of Christ richly dwell within you.

3. Be ministry-focused rather than self-focused.

4. Regularly express gratitude to God.

The final, important step in becoming more like Christ in your actions, your attitudes, and your affections is developing the attitude of gratitude.

God's Word as a whole, and the writings of the apostle Paul specifically, places a premium on developing and expressing gratitude to God. Focusing on God's graciousness in our lives has a way of riveting our attention "where Christ is" rather than on earth. And that is what being heavenly-minded is all about.

If someone were describing you, would they use the word *thankful* in their description? Are there frequent references to God's graciousness in your conversation with others? Do you regularly express thankfulness to God in your prayer time, or are your prayers characterized mainly by the words "give me"? If gratitude is so important, why do so many of us have a difficult time expressing it?

BARRIERS TO GRATITUDE

I have noticed five hindrances to expressing gratitude to God:

1. Materialism. Have you ever noticed that the more you have, the more you want? Solomon understood that truth. Remember Solomon? He was the world's richest man, yet he was never satisfied with his wealth. He wanted more. At the end of his life he observed, "He who loves money will not be satisfied with money, nor he who loves abundance with its income. This too is vanity" (Eccl. 5:10).

A well-known financial consultant, Ron Blue, once spoke at our church. He told a story about one of his clients. This man is a Christian multimillionaire. He owns properties all across the country and flies a luxurious jet. Recently, he had a meeting with a Saudi Arabian oil czar worth billions of dollars. The Christian millionaire told Blue, "Whenever I'm around that guy, I am intimidated." Isn't that funny? Here's a guy worth millions of dollars, yet he still doesn't feel like he has enough.

The person who believes that money will bring him happiness in life or who believes that money can protect him from all adversity in life will never feel like he has enough. Therefore, he will never be able to express thankfulness to God for what he has.

Have you ever seen one of those movies where people are stranded on a lifeboat out in the ocean? Without any fresh water to drink, and under the relentless heat of the sun, their temptation is to drink the salt water around them. The salt water cannot satisfy them. It only increases their thirst for water, and ultimately it will kill them.

So it is with materialism. The cruel truth about money is, not only does it not satisfy us, but it diverts our attention away from the One who can meet our needs.

2. Comparison. Closely related to materialism is what one of my seminary professors called "the favorite indoor sport of Christians"—comparison. Let's admit it. We are addicted to comparing ourselves to other people. We love to compare bank accounts, houses, clothes, cars, and children.

A group of pastors were attending their denomination's annual meeting and decided to do a little bragging about their Sunday morning attendance. When asked how many attended his church, one pastor answered, "Between four and five hundred." Everyone was impressed except one of the pastor's laymen who was also attending the conference and overheard his pastor's exaggerated claim. "Pastor, we only had seventy-five people present last week." "I know," the pastor admitted. "And seventy-five is between *four* and five hundred, isn't it?"

The problem with comparison is the same as with materialism. There will always be someone who has more than we do—someone with a bigger house, a larger home, a finer car, more gifted children, or a more sizable bank account. Comparison causes us to focus on what we don't have instead of being grateful for what we do have.

3. Pride. Another barrier to developing gratitude is the attitude of pride. Pride is the belief that one is responsible for the good things in his or her life. In my book *Choose Your Attitudes, Change Your Life*, I defined pride as "taking credit for your successes and blaming others for your failures." The Bible has numerous warnings against pride:

Pride and arrogance and the evil way, and the perverted mouth, I hate. (Prov. 8:13)

When pride comes, then comes dishonor, but with the humble is wisdom. (Prov. 11:2)

Pride goes before destruction, and a haughty spirit before stumbling. (Prov. 16:18)

All of you, clothe yourselves with humility toward one another, for God is opposed to the proud, but gives grace to the humble. (1 Pet. 5:5)

Why does God hate pride? God's plan is to draw people toward Himself. God wants a relationship with us. Pride drives us away from God, rather than drawing us closer to Him. I remember talking to a wealthy man about his need for Christ. His response? "I'm not opposed to religion. It is a good crutch for those who need it." Translation: "The only people who need God are the weak."

We all have a tendency toward pride. If someone compliments us on our appearance, our first thought may be, "Of course I look great. I work out every day." Or if someone admires our home, we may think, "Our home is the reward for our hard work and accomplishments. You could have a nice home, too, if you weren't such a loser." Maybe our children are exceptionally talented. Our unvoiced response? "How could they not be, considering who their parents are!"

In Ezekiel 28, we discover why God cast Lucifer (later known as Satan), His chief angel, from heaven: "You were blameless in your ways from the day you were created, until unrighteousness was found in you. . . . Your heart was lifted up because of your beauty; you corrupted your wisdom by reason of your splendor" (vv. 15, 17). What was Satan's problem? This most beautiful of God's creatures started taking credit for his beauty, rather than seeing it as an undeserved gift from God. Isaiah 14 records the next step in Satan's reasoning: "Since I am such a beautiful, powerful, and successful being, maybe I really don't need God. Better yet, maybe I can *be* God." When we begin to credit ourselves for any good thing in our lives, we are simply repeating the same mistake that ultimately drove Satan from the presence of God.

4. Loss of respect from others. I believe that some people are afraid that if they acknowledge God as the source of their achievements, they will come across as weak. I can identify with that concern.

Recently our church completed a high-attendance campaign that culminated on Easter. Our staff and laypeople worked hard to help us experience the highest attendance in our church's history. As a way of expressing gratitude toward our staff for their diligent work, I wanted to do something special for them. I planned to give each of them a gift certificate to a local department store and say a word of public commendation about them in my weekly newsletter. However, I have to admit that I hesitated for a moment. Would such recognition in some way diminish my position as pastor? Doesn't crediting other people with our successes make us appear expendable?

Then I remembered a plaque I had seen on the desk of former president Ronald Reagan one evening when a Secret Service agent was escorting my wife and me on a late-night tour of the White House. "There is no limit to the good a person can do if he is willing to let someone else take the credit."

As long as you have a life purpose that is larger than yourself (as we discussed in the last chapter), you will view gratitude as a way to enhance, rather than inhibit, your goals.

5. Failure to identify God's gifts. Sometimes life is moving so quickly that we fail to take time to identify the many ways God has blessed us. Those of you who are parents know how you feel after you have knocked yourself out doing something extra special for your children and they fail to show any appreciation. Then, as one last desperate act, you whine, "Aren't you going to say *something?*" Your child rolls his or her eyes and says in the most annoyed tone he or she can summon, "Thaaaank, youuuu," as if to say, "You moron. Don't you realize that your only reason for existing is to meet my every need?" You've been there before. How does such an episode make you feel?

I believe that our heavenly Father experiences that same emotion every time we fail to express thankfulness for the undeserved blessings we receive each day. How can you learn to make gratitude a part of your life and therefore become a heavenly-minded Christian?

Developing the Attitude of Gratitude

1. List God's blessings in your life. The other evening I asked our six-year-old daughter to pray before dinner. "What should I pray for?" she asked. "Thank God for all the things He has done for us," I advised. "Like *what?*" she persisted. I then started to list a number of things for which our family could be grateful. She agreed and proceeded to pray with great gusto. It wasn't that she did not want to thank God. She just had not taken the time to recall His blessings.

In 1 Corinthians 4:7, Paul asked a penetrating question: "For who regards you as superior? And what do you have that you did not receive? But if you did receive it, why do you boast as if you had not received it?" Paul asked the Corinthians to go through the same exercise that I encouraged my daughter to perform. "Do a mental inventory of every good thing in your life. Now, which of these things came from you and which came from God." Simple logic leads us to the conclusion that every good gift in life, beginning with life itself, comes from the hand of God.

Are you still identifying something to thank God for? Let me probe your thinking for a moment by listing several items that should be on every Christian's "Thank You" list:

Material blessings. I read a survey recently stating that 38 percent of Americans are dissatisfied with their current income—the highest number in thirty years. Maybe you are in that group. Or possibly you are neither particularly discouraged nor excited about your income. In either case, you might consider Paul's words in 1 Timothy 6: "For we have brought nothing into the world, so we cannot take anything out of it either. And if we have food and covering, with these we shall be content" (1 Tim. 6:7).

I want you to read those words again very slowly—especially the last sentence. Do you have a place to sleep tonight? Do you know where your next meal is coming from? If the answer to these questions is yes, Paul said you should be content. If you have any more than these basic items, you are way ahead of the game. From that perspective, we all have many things for which to be grateful.

Family. If you are married, do you regularly thank God for your mate? No, your spouse may not be all you want him or her to be—just like you are probably not everything your spouse would like you to be. But think for a moment what life would be like without your mate. In his book *Radical Commitment*, Vernon Grounds recounts this tragic episode from the life of writer Thomas Carlyle:

> Carlyle had married his secretary whom he dearly loved. But he was thoughtless, absorbed in his own interests and activities, treating his wife as if she were still his employee. Stricken with cancer, she was confined to bed for a long time before she died. After her funeral, Carlyle went back to his empty house. Disconsolate and grieving, he wandered around downstairs thinking about the woman he had loved.

After a while he went upstairs to her room and sat down in the chair beside the bed on which she had been lying for months. He realized with painful regret that he had not sat there very often during her long illness. He noticed her diary. While she was alive, he never would have read it, but now that she was gone he felt free to pick it up and thumb through its pages. One entry caught his eye: "Yesterday he spent an hour with me, and it was like being in heaven. I love him so much." He turned a few more pages and read, "I listened all day to hear his steps in the hall, but now it's late, and I guess he won't come to see me." Carlyle read a few more entries, then threw the book on the floor and rushed out through the rain back to the cemetery. He fell on his wife's grave in the mud, sobbing, "If only I had known. If only I had known."[1]

Unfortunately, Carlyle is like many people who take their mates for granted, rather than seeing them as gifts from the Lord.

The Bible also teaches that we should be grateful for our children. The psalmist declared, "Behold, children are a gift of the Lord; the fruit of the womb is a reward. Like arrows in the hand of a warrior, so are the children of one's youth" (Ps. 127:3–4). As we will see in the next chapter, it is natural to be exasperated with children at times. Yet God has endowed our children with unique qualities to enable them to achieve God's unique purpose for their lives. Learn to celebrate, rather than berate, those differences.

We should also thank God for our parents. Today, much of psychotherapy focuses on uncovering hurts of the past—especially those caused by our parents. Yet Proverbs 20:20 warns, "He who curses his father or his mother, his lamp will go out in time of darkness." Why should we be grateful for our parents? Psalm 139 teaches that every detail about your life was determined before you were born:

> For thou didst form my inward parts; Thou didst weave me in my mother's womb. I will give thanks to Thee, for I am

fearfully and wonderfully made. . . . My frame was not hidden from Thee, when I was made in secret, and skillfully wrought in the depths of the earth. Thine eyes have seen my unformed substance; and in Thy book they were all written, the days that were ordained for me, when as yet there was not one of them. (vv. 13–16, KJV)

If God designed every part of your anatomy ahead of time, it means that He must have selected your parents (with their unique genes) for you. Thus, our parents are a very real part of God's sovereign plan for our lives.

Your church. Someone has commented that the church is a lot like Noah's ark—if it were not for the storm on the outside, you could not stand the stench on the inside. That may sound cynical to some, but if you have been part of a local church for any period of time, you understand the point. Being in a church can be messy at times. Disputes and dissension are sometimes an unpleasant part of congregational life.

Yet I often hear this comment from Christians who have experienced a tragedy in their life: "I am so grateful for the way our church family has stood by us. I don't know how people make it without a church." No, your church may not be perfect. But what would your life be like without it? Again, the psalmist encouraged us to "enter His gates with thanksgiving" (Ps. 100:4). When you walk through the doors of your church this Sunday, take time to thank God for your church. It will help remove some of the stench.

Answered prayer. We are often quick to ask God for something, but not quite so quick to thank Him for His answer. I like the way *The Living Bible* paraphrases Philippians 4:6: "Don't worry about anything; instead, pray about everything; tell God your needs *and don't forget to thank him for his answers*" (emphasis mine). Maybe God doesn't always perform like you think He should. But are you willing to thank Him for the times He has granted your requests? And are you willing to trust that the Father knows best when He says "no" or "wait"?

Our problems. Brian Harbour tells the story of a second-grader named David. He was bumped while getting on the school bus and suffered a scratch down the side of his face. At recess he collided with another boy and two of his teeth were knocked loose. At noon, while sliding on the ice, he fell and broke his wrist. The school called David's father, who took him to the hospital. On the way to the hospital, his father noticed David clutching something in his hand. "What do you have in your hand?" "This is a quarter. I found it on the ground when I fell and broke my wrist. This is the first quarter I ever found. Boy, is this my lucky day!"[2]

Paul was a living example of what it means to thank God in spite of your problems. At the beginning of the chapter, I noted the references to "thanksgiving" and "gratitude" in the Book of Colossians. Paul's attitude was remarkable when you consider his circumstances when he penned this letter. He was in prison, facing what could have been his execution. Yet, he was convinced God was in control. That assurance allowed him to continually express gratitude to God.

Our salvation. At the top of the list of God's undeserved gifts in our life is salvation from our sins. The Bible teaches that we were a condemned race, headed for an eternity of separation from God. Yet "while we were still helpless, at the right time Christ died for the ungodly. . . . But God demonstrates His own love toward us, in that while we were yet sinners, Christ died for us" (Rom. 5:6, 8).

Think for a moment about what your life was like (or would have been like) without Jesus Christ. Review in your mind the supernatural events that led you to become a Christian. It may have been a dramatic event in your life that brought you to Christ. It may have been the deep concern of a Christian friend. It may have been the loving instruction and prayers of a parent. Pause to express your appreciation to God for intervening in your life.

The most important step in developing gratitude in your life is to identify God's blessings in your life. As we bring this chapter to a close, let me briefly describe four other steps that will help you in this process.

2. *Keep a written record of answered prayer in your life.* In each of my books, I somewhere mention the importance of keeping a spiritual journal. This practice has revolutionized my spiritual life. A spiritual journal is not a diary. Instead of being a detailed record of your day-to-day activities, a spiritual journal records how God is working in your life. What problems are you struggling with? What are you asking God to do in your life? What truth is God teaching you in your life? Which prayers has He answered? To which prayers has God said no?

While I try to write one page in my journal each day after I pray and read the Bible, I sometimes miss a day or two. That's all right. The important thing is that I am able to look back over the years and see how God has directed my life. I find a journal is especially helpful during times of anxiety or discouragement. To be able to look back and see how God has intervened in my life in the past gives me courage to face my present circumstances. It also gives me a number of things for which to thank God.

Throughout the Old Testament, God encouraged the Israelites to remember His faithfulness to them in the past: through the exodus, the parting of the Red Sea, the miraculous provisions in the wilderness, and the entry into the promised land. He even designed ceremonies and instructed Moses to compose songs that would remind the Israelites of these signal events. Why? Recalling God's faithfulness in the past would provide the courage and the motivation to obey God in the future. In the same way, a daily journal can remind you of specific answers to prayer for which to thank God.

3. Begin and end every day expressing gratitude to God. It is easy for us to make "give me" our first words to God. However, if you will discipline yourself to begin each day by thanking God for one of His provisions in your life, you will find it changes your whole attitude for the entire day.

"Lord, thank You for the job You have given me that provides for my needs and the needs of my family."

"Lord, thank You for my family. They are an undeserved gift from You."

"Lord, thank You for allowing me to live through the night and giving me another day to serve You."

Likewise, if you will make thanking God your last act before you drift off to sleep each evening, you will find yourself experiencing a new level of rest during the night.

4. Express thanks to others who have made a significant difference in your life. Ultimately, all our blessings come from God. James said, "Every good thing bestowed and every perfect gift is from above, coming down from the Father of lights" (1:17). Yet many times God blesses through other people. Identifying and thanking those whom He has used is one way to express gratitude to God.

In my life, there have been two men who have played critical roles in my ministry. Recently I sat down and wrote a letter to one of those mentors, thanking him for the way he has influenced my life. "I have thought of you many times this year—during a deacon's meeting, a staff meeting, or even a funeral—and have thanked God that I had you to teach me and model for me how to pastor a church."

Who has made a difference in your life? Do you realize that it is God who has placed those people in your life? Take a moment to call them on the phone or write them a note to express your appreciation for them.

5. Demonstrate your gratitude to God in practical ways. When we moved to our present church, we did not have long to purchase a house. After a whirlwind tour by the real estate agent, we settled on a house where we felt most comfortable. We were proud of our ability to make a decision and complete the transaction so quickly. At my first staff meeting, someone asked the location of our new house. When I told him, he said, "Oh, I know that house well. Several years ago, I helped the previous owner bail water out of it during the flood. The water was up to my knees." Our house was located near a creek, and when the rain came, the creek overflowed its banks.

In Colossians 2:7 Paul said that a heavenly-minded Christian's life should be "overflowing with gratitude." In other words, if our lives are characterized by thanksgiving, that gratitude will splash over onto those around us. You can't contain genuine gratitude to God. It will always affect those around you. Let me suggest several practical ways you can channel your gratitude into meaningful action.

Are you grateful to God for your material blessings? Why not express that gratitude by giving an unexpected cash gift to a deserving person like a missionary or someone you know who could use it?

Are you grateful for your family? If you are a man, why not tell your wife that you will take care of the kids all day this Saturday so that she can do anything she would like? If you are a woman, why not make a list of the five things you most appreciate about your husband and share them with him tonight after the kids are asleep?

Are you thankful for your church? Why not write the pastor a note of encouragement, telling him of your gratitude for his leadership and assuring him of your prayers.

Every Friday evening an old man walks down a Florida beach. Except for a few joggers and strollers, the man is all alone. In his hand he carries a bucket of shrimp—not for him or the fish, but for the sea gulls. He walks out to the end of the pier and waits.

Soon the sky becomes filled with screeching birds. For the next half hour, the old man stands on the pier feeding the gulls until his bucket is empty. Even after the food is consumed, the gulls remain. They linger on the pier; they perch on his hat. They are sharing a moment of fellowship together. The weekly ritual is the man's way of saying thank you. The old man's name is Eddie Rickenbacker, the World War II hero who was reported missing at sea in October of 1942. He had been dispatched to deliver a message to General Douglas MacArthur. Somewhere over the South Pacific, the crew lost its way, and the plane ran out of fuel and crashed into the ocean. The eight crew members survived the crash. After eight days of fighting against the weather, the sharks, and the sun, their provisions were expended. All hope was gone. After a brief time of prayer, they drifted off to sleep in the life rafts.

Then the sea gull came. It landed on Rickenbacker's hat. He was able to catch the gull, eat its flesh, and use the intestines for fish bait. Rickenbacker and his crew survived. All because of a sea gull that "mysteriously" appeared out of nowhere. So every Friday evening, the old captain walks down that lonesome pier to meet his friends with a bucket filled with shrimp and his heart filled with gratitude.[3]

Rickenbacker's story reminds us that if our lives are truly overflowing with gratitude, we will find tangible ways to express our appreciation to others.

❋

ACTION STEPS

1. Be honest with yourself. What are you really depending on to bring you happiness and security in life? _____

_____

_____

2. One enemy of gratitude is comparison to other people. What aspects of your life are you most tempted to compare? _____

_____

_____

3. Think about the accomplishment in your life of which you are most proud. Relate how another person and/or God helped you in reaching that goal. _____

_____

_____

4. List three instances in which God supernaturally intervened in your life. Pause right now to thank Him for His work. _____

_____

_____

5. Begin keeping a spiritual journal. Start with a goal of writing in it three times a week.

6. Memorize Colossians 3:17.

The Evidence of Being Heavenly-Minded

Wives, be subject to your husbands, as is fitting in the Lord. Husbands love your wives, and do not be embittered against them. Children, be obedient to your parents in all things, for this is well pleasing to the Lord. Fathers, do not exasperate your children, that they may not lose heart. Slaves, in all things obey those who are your masters on earth, not with external service, as those who merely please men, but with sincerity of heart, fearing the Lord. Whatever you do, do your work heartily as for the Lord rather than for men; knowing that from the Lord you will receive the reward of the inheritance. It is the Lord Christ whom you serve. For he who does wrong will receive the consequences of the wrong which he has done, and that without partiality. Masters, grant to your slaves justice and fairness, knowing that you too have a Master in heaven.

— COLOSSIANS 3:18–4:1

Does Your Home Work?

A man passing through the Dallas/Fort Worth Airport was concerned that he might miss his plane. Unfortunately, he had left his watch at home and could not find a clock on the wall. He found a halfway friendly face in the sea of people hurrying through the terminal and asked, "Can you please tell me what time it is?" The stranger replied, "Of course." He set down the two large suitcases he was carrying, looked at his watch and said, "It is exactly 6:43 P.M. The temperature is seventy-eight degrees and it should rain tomorrow. Furthermore, the sky is clear in Hong Kong and there the temperature is forty-five degrees. In London the barometer is 30.15 and dropping."

The man was astonished. "Your watch told you all of that?"

"Sure did. I invented this watch myself and it is the only one of its kind in the world."

"I will pay you four thousand dollars for the watch right now."

"Oh, no," the man responded. "I was planning on giving this watch to my son when he graduates from college."

"All right, I'll give you *ten* thousand dollars."

The man thought for a moment and replied, "It's yours."

After receiving the money, the stranger removed the watch and gave it to the man. The man was ecstatic over his purchase. He strapped the watch on his wrist, expressed his thanks, and turned to walk away.

"Wait just a moment," the stranger said. With a giant smile he handed the man the two heavy suitcases he had been carrying. "Don't forget the batteries."[1]

We have the tendency to make simple things unnecessarily complex. I believe that is certainly true about marriage and parenting. There are countless books, tapes, and seminars about the home. As a pastor, I appreciate any help these tools can give people in building homes that will survive the assaults of a fallen world. Yet I am afraid the volume of material available about the family has given people the impression that building a successful family is impossibly complex. The truth is that while maintaining a successful family is not easy—it takes work—it is simple. In just four short verses in Colossians 3, Paul explained the basic ingredients necessary for a successful home.

How do you know if you are becoming like Christ? What is the test of whether or not you have laid aside wrong thoughts and behavior and put on the actions and attitudes described in verses 5–14? In this final section of Colossians 3, Paul says the test of your sanctification (the theological term for becoming like Jesus Christ) is how you behave at home and at work. Billy Graham once said, "The true test of the Christian is the way he lives at home." Paul said the same thing in Colossians 3:18–21: "Wives, be subject to your husbands, as is fitting in the Lord.

Husbands, love your wives, and do not be embittered against them. Children, be obedient to your parents in all things, for this is well-pleasing to the Lord. Fathers, do not exasperate your children, that they may not lose heart."

Paul did not give a detailed instruction manual for building a successful family. Instead, Paul explained how to know whether or not you have truly "set your minds on the things above." Are you really becoming like Christ Jesus? Then, here's the test:

➤ Wives, are you submissive to your husbands—even when you don't want to be?
➤ Husbands, do you sacrificially love your wives, like Christ loves us?
➤ Children, do you obey your parents?
➤ Parents, do you encourage your children?

These are the practical tests of whether or not you are like Jesus Christ.

THE SERMON NO ONE WANTS TO HEAR

Last month I performed a wedding ceremony. After my touching words about the supremacy of love (borrowed heavily from 1 Cor. 13), we got down to the business of the vows. I asked the bride, "Do you _____ promise to love and obey _____ until death alone shall part you?" She responded, "I do." I asked the groom if he would love his bride with a sacrificial love, just as Christ loved us. He also agreed. They exchanged rings, we prayed, I pronounced them husband and wife, and they departed.

After the ceremony, the grandmother of the bride approached me. "Pastor, that was a beautiful ceremony. But I want you to know that if you had asked me the same question you asked my granddaughter, I would have answered, 'Absolutely not!'"

That grandmother voiced an opinion that many women have whenever they hear a sermon on submission. I am amazed how many Christian women are ready to jettison their belief in the inspiration of Scripture when it comes to verses like Colossians 3:18 ("Wives, be subject to your husbands, as is fitting in the Lord") or Ephesians 5:22 ("Wives, be subject to your own husbands, as to the Lord"). Paul's status suddenly changes from "God's chosen apostle" to "typical male chauvinist pig."

Unfortunately, pastors are partly to blame for this attitude. Many Bible teachers have twisted Paul's words about submission to say something the apostle never intended to communicate. Nowhere does the Bible ever imply that women are inferior to men. In fact, the New Testament elevated women to a position of prominence that was unique to the culture of the New Testament world.

The word *submit* comes from a military term that means "to arrange under rank." We submit to another person based on that person's position, not his personality or ability. As those in the military say, "You salute the uniform, not the person in the uniform." My brother is a policeman in Dallas, Texas. When he signals for a motorist to pull over, why does the motorist obey him? The motorist may be superior to my brother in intellect and ability. Yet the citizen submits to my brother's instructions because of the office my brother holds. Such a chain of command is vital to a civilized society. In fact, God has arranged it so that all of us are under someone else's authority:

➤ Employees are under the authority of their employers (see Col. 3:22).

➤ Citizens are under the authority of the government (see Rom. 13:1).

➤ Church members are under the authority of the spiritual leaders in the congregation (see Heb. 13:17).

➢ Children are under the authority of their parents (see Eph. 6:1).

➢ Wives are under the authority of their husbands (see Col. 3:18).

Why has God arranged His world like this? Let me suggest four reasons.

1. Submitting to authority teaches us obedience to God. The bottom-line issue in the Christian life is not doctrine or feeling, but obedience to God. Jesus said, "If you love Me, you will keep My commandments" (John 14:15). Yet every parent knows that obedience is not an attitude that is instantly imparted to a child. If it were, our lives would be so much easier! No, obedience must be learned. We have to teach our children over and over the importance of obeying our instruction.

So it is with our relationship with God. Our natural inclination is not to obey God, but to rebel against God (see Rom. 3:10–12). We must learn how to be obedient to His will. And one way God teaches us to obey Him is by placing us under someone else's authority. Being submissive to a husband, parent, employee, or government official allows me to practice obeying when I don't feel like obeying or when I don't understand why I should obey.

One of the most fascinating verses in the New Testament to me is Hebrews 5:8. In describing Jesus Christ, the writer of Hebrews said, "Although He was a Son, He learned obedience from the things which He suffered." Is the verse implying that Jesus was inferior to God the Father? That would be heresy. The Bible teaches that Jesus is equal to God. Yet Jesus voluntarily gave up His divine rights as God and humbled Himself by being obedient to God's will for His life (see Phil. 2:5–9).

In the same way, a marriage is a union between two equals. Before marriage, the man and woman are equal in their position. I often remind single adults who are dating that there is no such thing as "submission" in dating. The man has no authority over the woman. In fact, in many situations, the woman may be superior in intellect and ability. However, when two people are married, something changes. The wife does not suddenly become inferior to the man; she does not "give up" her personality and her gifts. She may *still* be superior to her husband in intellect and ability. Yet Paul encouraged wives to voluntarily submit to the authority of their husbands—just as Jesus voluntarily submitted to the authority of God the Father—so that they can learn the invaluable attitude of obedience to God.

2. *Submitting to authority provides orderliness.* During the period in Israel's history in which there was no king, we find these words: "In those days there was no king in Israel; everyone did what was right in his own eyes" (Judg. 21:25). That is the prescription for chaos in any organization. Just imagine a world in which:

> *There were no policemen.*
> *Everyone was just encouraged to "do the right thing."*

> *Your company had no supervisors.*
> *Employees reported in and left when they felt like it.*

> *The country had no Internal Revenue Service.*
> *Everyone sent the government what they felt they could afford.*

Sure, all the above scenarios are appealing. Yet, they would result in the disintegration of our nation. In any organization, there must be someone who has the final say. As Adrian Rogers often says, "Anything with more than one head is a freak; and anything with no head is dead!"

3. *Submitting to authority frees us from unnecessary worry.* Someone has defined worry as "assuming responsibility for things God never intended for you to have." A few

weeks ago a man visited with me about the anxiety he was experiencing at work. His boss was illegally evading taxes. "What should I do?" he asked. "Have you shared with your boss your concerns?" He told me he had, but his boss was unresponsive. "Then do your job as well as you can and stop worrying. This is not your responsibility," I advised.

Authority and responsibility go hand in hand. You can't have authority without responsibility. If the husband is the head of the family, then he is also responsible for the family. The wife can experience freedom from worry because she is not ultimately responsible for what happens to the family—her husband is. And God promises to protect the woman who submits to her husband.

Peter said in his epistle: "In the same way, you wives, be submissive to your own husbands. . . . For in this way in former times the holy women also, who hoped in God, used to adorn themselves, being submissive to their own husbands. Thus Sarah obeyed Abraham, calling him lord, and you have become her children if you do what is right without being frightened by any fear" (1 Pet. 3:1, 5–6).

You probably remember the story about Abraham, Sarah, and Abimelech (Gen. 20). Abraham and his wife were traveling through some dangerous territory. Abraham was afraid that King Abimelech, enchanted by Sarah's beauty, might take her for himself and kill Abraham. So Abraham devised a plan. He instructed Sarah to say she was his sister (this was a half-truth since she really was his half-sister) so that Abimelech would not kill him. Let's stop here for a moment and admit that Abraham was not exactly a contender for the "Husband of the Year" award. He was willing to give away his wife to save his own skin! Yet, when Abimelech took Sarah for himself, God supernaturally protected her. We can argue all day whether or not Sarah should have told the half-truth. But don't miss the main point. God honored Sarah's obedience to a less-than-deserving husband.

We need to present a balancing truth here. If anyone in authority ever asks us to directly disobey God's Word, we are never to submit. If a wife, child, employee, citizen, or church member is ever instructed to violate God's command, he must respectfully resist. Peter said, "We must obey God rather than men" (Acts 5:29). But outside of that situation, whenever we submit to the authority God has placed over us, we can be assured of His divine protection. And we can be free from worrying about the consequences of our obedience.

4. Submitting to authority gives us direction in life. When I was a youth minister, teenagers would often ask me which college they should attend, whom they should date, or what career they should pursue. My first response was always the same. "What do your parents say?" Their response was also always the same. They would look at me as if I were crazy. "What does that have to do with it?" I would then ask, "Do you want to know God's answer to your question?"

"Of course."

"How do you expect God to show you the answer?"

Sometimes the reply would be, "Reading my Bible" or "Praying." Most of the time the answer was a shrug of the shoulders.

I would then explain to them that most probably they would not find the name of their mate in the Bible (unless it was Ruth, Esther, or Noah). Nor would God probably shout the name of their college down from heaven. Instead, God often uses the authority figures He has placed over us to communicate His direction to us.

The same principle is true in the marriage relationship. God often communicates direction for a family—where to live, what church to attend, how to discipline children— through the husband. This does not mean that the husband is to be a dictator. If he is a wise husband, he will value the opinions and insights of his wife. And hopefully, the wife will be so convinced of her husband's love and concern for her welfare that she will voluntarily submit to his authority. That thought leads us to the second responsibility discussed in Colossians 3.

How to Keep the Home Fires Burning

Those who claim that Paul was prejudiced against women usually don't read Colossians 3:19: "Husbands, love your wives, and do not be embittered against them." In the Greek culture, the husband had no obligations. He was free to come and go as he pleased. The idea that a husband would also have a responsibility in the home was a revolutionary concept in Paul's day. Yet, just as a wife's submission to her husband is a reflection of Christ's character, so is a husband's sacrificial love for his wife. The test of a wife's Christlikeness is submission; the test of a husband's Christlikeness is his sacrificial love.

Paul expanded on this idea in his Letter to the Ephesians: "Husbands, love your wives, just as Christ also loved the church and gave Himself up for her. . . . So husbands ought also to love their own wives as their own bodies" (5:25, 28). Husbands, do your actions, affections, and attitudes reflect those of Jesus Christ? If so, you will be regularly expressing unselfish and sacrificial love for your mate.

Allow me to suggest several practical ways husbands can demonstrate a sacrificial love for their spouses:

1. *Do something nice and unexpected for your wife.* When was the last time you surprised your wife by doing some-

thing kind and unexpected? You might say: "Well, I went to work today to provide for our food and shelter." Sorry, that doesn't count. Those things come under the heading of "expected." Here are several suggestions you might consider.

➤ Offer to take care of dinner tonight. You can either cook or take the family out.

➤ Hire a cleaning service for a day to take care of all the gritty household chores—cleaning bathrooms, waxing floors, vacuuming the carpets. If you can't afford to hire someone, have your kids assist you in the job. (On second thought, stick with the cleaning service!)

➤ Arrange for your wife to be able to visit her family. Take care of the necessary travel arrangements or child care.

➤ Tell your wife that this Saturday belongs to her. You will gladly take her wherever she wishes to go (yes, including the mall). Now that's sacrificial love!

2. Be concerned with your wife's physical, emotional, and spiritual needs. When Paul told the husbands in Ephesus to love their wives as they do themselves, he was encouraging men to be just as concerned about meeting their wives' needs as they are about satisfying their own. However, to be able to meet my wife's needs, I must first understand what they are! And I must accept that her needs are far different than mine.

My wife likes Italian food; I prefer Mexican. She likes it warmer in the house; I like it cooler. Husbands and wives have different physical needs, including sexual needs. This week I read an interesting survey concerning women's attitudes toward sex. *Redbook* magazine asked women which of seven activities would bring them the most pleasure in life. The result? Twenty-nine percent of the women rated "relaxing on a beautiful tropical beach" as the most pleasurable activity and 28 percent picked "having a romantic dinner with your husband or boyfriend." Only 9 percent ranked "having sex" as the most pleasurable activity. In fact, for these women sex barely ranked above "a piece of chocolate cake with whipped cream and hot fudge" (9 percent vs. 8 percent).[2] Yet if you conducted that same survey among five hundred men, I can guarantee you the results would be vastly different!

A husband who demonstrates sacrificial love for his wife will also be concerned with meeting her emotional needs. I have discovered that my wife Amy needs me to compliment her for those areas about which she feels unsure. An encouraging word about her clothes, parenting skills, or cooking many times gives her the boost she needs.

She also needs time each day for me to give her my undivided attention. When I come home I am usually wrung out. I don't want to talk to anyone—I just want to sit and vegetate for a while. But Amy has been busy all day taking care of two hyperactive preschoolers. She desires adult conversation.

A husband who truly loves his wife will be concerned about her spiritual needs. I recently visited with a woman whose family had been visiting our church. She and her three children desperately wanted to join our fellowship. But her husband came from a different denomination. He was looking for a more "spirit-filled" (i.e., charismatic) church. The result was that the family continued church-hopping wherever they were. She had a deep desire to join a church where she could develop a network of friends and her children could be grounded in the Christian faith. But he was more concerned about his spiritual needs than those of his family. A heavenly-minded husband will be more interested in his wife's needs than his own.

3. Learn to forgive your spouse instantly. Paul added a word to his command to husbands. He said, "Do not be embittered against them." Nothing destroys a relationship faster than bitterness. Hebrews 12:15 warns: "See to it that no one comes short of the grace of God; that no root of bitterness springing up causes trouble, and by it many be defiled." Bitterness is like a weed that springs up overnight and chokes out the love of a relationship. As a pastor, I have seen bitterness destroy churches, businesses, and marriages. I know men and women who have been bitter toward their spouses about an event that occurred years ago. It may be something as traumatic as an affair or something as trivial as a forgotten anniversary. But they have allowed their unresolved anger to completely extinguish their love for their spouse.

What is the answer to anger we feel toward those who have mistreated us? Paul said, "Be kind to one another, tenderhearted, forgiving each other, just as God in Christ also has forgiven you" (Eph. 4:32). The antidote for bitterness is forgiveness. The word *forgive* literally means "to release." At some point in a marriage, your spouse is going to offend you or hurt you deeply. You cannot control what your mate does to you. But you can choose how you will respond to that offense. You can either hold on to it, or you can choose to release it. Paul said that a heavenly-minded Christian is one who releases the offenses of his mate on the basis of how God has forgiven him.

Order in the House

Paul's letter to the Colossians was probably read out loud to the entire congregation. No doubt, there were children present in the audience to hear the apostle's instructions. I think it is significant that Paul did not leave out the children in his discourse. He had an important word for them as well: "Children, be obedient to your parents in all things, for this is well-pleasing to the Lord" (3:20). The test of a wife's Christlikeness is her voluntary submission to her husband. The test of a husband's Christlikeness is his sacrificial love for his wife. Now, Paul adds that if a child has truly set his mind on "the things above," he will be obedient to his parents "in all things."

Paul used a different word in explaining a wife's responsibility and a child's responsibility in the home. The word used to describe a wife's submission to her husband carries the idea of voluntary submission. The husband is never commanded to force her submission. She chooses to submit, out of deference to Jesus Christ.

On the other hand, children are commanded to "obey" their parents "in all things." Let me make two observations about this simple command. First, it is made to children, not adults. Children living at home are under the authority of their parents. Even though the word *obey* is different from the word *submit*, the reasons for obeying one's parents are the same as submission to authority (see above section). However, when a child marries and leaves home, he is no longer under the direct authority of his parents.

Not long ago, a young man called me for advice. He had been offered a fabulous job in another city. His young family was excited about the move, but his dad (who lived in the same city) could not bear to see his son leave. He was adamantly opposed to his son's move. He even quoted this passage from Colossians as "proof" that his son should obey him and not accept the new position.

While talking to the young man, I had him turn in his Bible to Genesis 2:24: "For this cause a man shall leave his father and his mother, and shall cleave to his wife; and they shall become one flesh." I explained that a successful marriage requires physically and emotionally leaving our parents. I have seen many marriages suffer unnecessary stress because of a failure to sever ties to parents. I am not suggesting that we should no longer love our parents, visit them, or seek their advice. We should always honor our parents. But the strict command to obey is reserved for single children still living in the home.

The second observation is that the phrase "in all things" must be qualified. Paul is trying to communicate that a child's obedience is not to be arbitrary ("I will clean up my room if I feel like it"). What if Jesus had chosen to obey His Father in everything, except the one thing He really did not want to do—the cross?

Yet a child is never to violate God's direct commands in order to obey his parents. There may come a time when a child or teenager must disobey his parents (and suffer the resulting consequences) in order to follow Christ. Jesus said, "If anyone comes to Me, and does not hate his own father and mother and wife and children and brothers and sisters, yes, and even his own life, he cannot be My disciple" (Luke 14:26). Jesus was not suggesting that we need to harbor emotional hatred against our parents. The word translated "hate" carries the idea of making a choice (see Rom. 9:13 where God says, "Jacob I loved; Esau I hated"). Jesus is simply saying that if there ever is any choice between obeying one's parents or obeying Christ, a child is always commanded to obey Christ.

Train Up a Child

Paul's final word about the home is addressed to parents: "Fathers, do not exasperate your children, that they may not lose heart" (3:21). While specifically addressing the father, most commentators agree Paul had both parents in mind. Parents are warned against so frustrating or embittering their children that they become discouraged.

One way parents frustrate their children is by *nagging* them—especially about insignificant things. The parent who is always criticizing his child ("Why is your room always a mess?" or "Why can't you do anything right?") will eventually cause the child to give up or "lose heart."

A second way parents embitter their children is by *unfavorable comparison* to other children or siblings. "Why can't you be more like_____?" Our children's self-esteem is fragile. James Dobson said, "It is a wise adult who understands that self-esteem is the most fragile characteristic in human nature, and once broken, its reconstruction is more difficult than repairing Humpty Dumpty."[3]

A third way we frustrate children is through *inconsistency in our discipline*. For example, a couple in one of my former churches used to constantly send mixed signals to their six-year-old son. We might be out at a restaurant with this family, and the boy would misbehave. On one occasion, the parents laughed at their son's antics. The next time he did something almost identical, he was taken outside and walloped. Such "discipline" is comparable to a rider who sticks his spurs into the side of his horse, while at the same time pulling back on the reins. The horse will eventually become frustrated and "lose heart."

Other times children become the pawns in marital squabbles. A mother tells her teenage daughter that she is grounded next Friday for breaking curfew. What does the daughter do? She asks Dad if she can go out Friday night. Dad is ticked off at Mom about something else and so, to get under Mom's skin, he says yes. Immediately, World War III begins. Unfortunately, the child is the one who suffers the most in such a dispute.

A heavenly-minded parent not only refrains from discouraging his children, he also works to nurture his children. In Ephesians 6:4 Paul teaches: "And, fathers, do not provoke your children to anger; but bring them up in the discipline and instruction of the Lord." The test of whether or not a parent has "set his mind on the things above" is his commitment to developing his child's relationship with God. In my book *Guilt-Free Living*, I suggest several responsibilities parents have toward their children:

1. We should dedicate our children to God. Just as Hannah dedicated Samuel to the Lord, we need to give our children totally to God. To dedicate our children to the Lord means to give up our dreams for our children and make it our goal to help our children fulfill God's plan for their lives.

2. We should encourage our children to become Christians. Yes, ultimately the child must decide for himself about accepting Christ. But we can greatly influence that decision. How? First, we can pray daily for the salvation of our children. Second, we can continually impress (without nagging) upon them the importance of being a Christian. And third, we can set definite times to share the gospel with our children and lead them to faith in Christ.

3. We should impart spiritual values to our children. In chapter 9, we talked about being "ministry-focused" in our lives. The Great Commission must begin with our family. Our children are our first and most important discipleship projects. In Deuteronomy 6:4–7, Moses commanded:

> Hear, O Israel! The Lord is our God, the Lord is one! And you shall love the Lord your God with all your heart and with all your soul and with all your might. And these words, which I am commanding you today, shall be on your heart; and you shall teach them diligently to your sons and shall talk of them when you sit in your house and when you walk by the way and when you lie down and when you rise up.

I notice two things about Moses' command. First, parents are to be totally committed to making spiritual truth a priority in their home. He says parents are to teach their children about God diligently. The word *diligently* literally means "at early dawn." In other words, spiritual instruction is to take priority over Little League, gymnastics, scholastic achievement. Is that the case in your home?

Moses said spiritual instruction is to take place in the natural course of life. He did not limit the communication of spiritual truth to Sunday mornings from 11:00 A.M. until noon. Nor did he suggest that we gather our children into the living room once a week, open our dusty family Bible, and say, "Now, kids, here is a word from God." Moses had a more effective way to teach our children. He said we are to teach our children when we sit down at a meal, when we travel in the car, and before we go to bed at night. There are many teachable moments in the normal flow of life when we can make a deep impression on our child:

> when they are deeply hurt by a friend;
> when we are facing financial difficulty and must depend on God;
> when God answers a specific prayer request;
> when someone reaps the consequences of their sin;
> when a loved one dies.

A parent who is heavenly-minded will seize those moments to draw his children closer to God.

Annis Duff once wrote, "Successful family living strikes me as being in many ways rather like playing chamber music. Each member of the ensemble has his own skills, but the grace and strength and sweetness of the performance come from everyone's willingness to subordinate individual virtuosity and personal ambition to the requirements of balance and blend."[4] Is the music emanating from your home beautiful or dissonant? How are you doing at the individual part you have been given to perform? Are you determined to play it your way, or to blend in with the other players? Your answer to those questions will reveal whether you are truly a heavenly-minded Christian.

✳

Action Steps

1. In this chapter we have looked at the first test of whether or not we are heavenly-minded Christians: our behavior at home. How do you measure up? Rate yourself on a scale of 1–5 (5 being the highest) :

Wives (submission)	1 2 3 4 5
Husbands (sacrificial love)	1 2 3 4 5
Children (obedience)	1 2 3 4 5
Parents (spiritual instruction)	1 2 3 4 5

2. If you are a wife, identify an area in which you need to be more submissive to your husband. If you are a husband, why might your wife have difficulty voluntarily submitting to your authority? Is there something you could do differently? _____

_____

_____

_____

3. If you are a wife, what would be the most loving thing your husband could do for you this week? _____

_____

_____

In a nonthreatening and nonaccusatory way, see if there is not an opportunity for you to suggest that to him this week. "Honey, do you know what would mean so much to me? If sometime you would unexpectedly . . ."

4. If you are a husband, identify the greatest specific need your wife has in the following areas:

Physical: _____

Emotional: _____

Spiritual: _____

Look for opportunities this week to meet those needs.

5. How would your children rate you as a parent in the following areas (5 being the highest):

Consistency in discipline	1 2 3 4 5
Fairness in discipline	1 2 3 4 5
Encouraging remarks	1 2 3 4 5
Patience	1 2 3 4 5
Open display of affection	1 2 3 4 5

6. Identify three steps of action you can take to make the spiritual instruction of your children a priority in your house. _____

_____

_____

_____

7. Memorize Colossians 3:18–21.

TWELVE

Who's the Boss?

In his book *Lyrics*, the great lyricist Oscar Hammerstein writes of seeing a photograph of the top of the Statue of Liberty taken from a helicopter. Hammerstein relates his surprise at seeing the tremendous amount of effort expended on the great lady's hair.

When the designer Bartholdi was performing his work, he had no idea that one hundred years later a device would be invented that would allow a photographer to fly above the head of his creation and snap a picture.

Hammerstein then added the obvious moral of the lesson, "When you are creating a work of art, or any other kind of work, finish the job off perfectly. You never know when a helicopter or some other instrument not at the moment invented, may come along and find you out."

Hammerstein's story is a powerful motivation to do one's work with excellence. But the apostle Paul offered an even stronger incentive to perform our work well in Colossians 3:22–4:1:

> Slaves, in all things obey those who are your masters on earth, not with external service, as those who merely please men, but with sincerity of heart, fearing the Lord. Whatever you do, do your work heartily, as for the Lord rather than for men; knowing that from the Lord you will receive the reward of the inheritance. It is the Lord Christ whom you serve. For he who does wrong will receive the consequences of the wrong which he has done, and that without partiality. Masters, grant to your slaves justice and fairness, knowing that you too have a Master in heaven.

Remember that in this section of Colossians 3, Paul was explaining the results of being a heavenly-minded Christian. If you are allowing your affections, attitudes, and actions to be conformed to those of Jesus Christ, there will be demonstrable evidence of that change in two areas: your home and your work. Why did Paul select these two areas? I think one reason is because of the amount of time we spend both in our home and at work. If we are not at one place, we are usually at the other. Some estimates say that Americans spend 60 percent of their time at the workplace.

Another reason Paul focused on the home and the workplace as proving grounds for our Christianity is the amount of natural friction we encounter in both places. Think about the two areas of life where you face the greatest challenges. I would imagine your home and your job are at the top of the list. Molding two lives together in a marriage, nurturing children who love God, submitting to employers who are unfair and/or incompetent, and treating employees with fairness and compassion are enough to tax anyone's faith!

This section of Colossians 3 describes a very practical way for both employees and employers to demonstrate their Christianity in the workplace.

Take This Job and . . . Love It!

The relationship between masters and slaves was so relevant to the Colossian church that Paul devoted more space to this issue than to any other in Colossians 3. Today, nearly two thousand years later, it is obvious that our culture has changed dramatically. No longer do we live under a master-slave arrangement. Nevertheless, we still find ourselves spending as much time at work as we do at home. How should our relationship with Christ impact our work? Let me suggest three principles I find in Colossians 3:22–25.

1. We are to obey our employers just as we obey Christ. We need to understand something about the culture in which Paul wrote to fully appreciate the impact his words must have had on his audience. By some estimates there were 60 million slaves in the Roman Empire during the time of Paul—about one-half of the population. Chances are there were probably more slaves in the church at Colossae than masters. Picture all of the slaves (who were allowed to attend) seated in the church alongside their masters to eagerly receive this letter of instruction from the great apostle. They were eagerly waiting to hear what Paul had to say to them about the master-slave relationship. I imagine that some of the slaves secretly hoped that the apostle would command the masters to free their slaves. After all, a minute or two earlier they had heard these words from Paul's pen: "There is no distinction between Greek and Jew, circumcised and uncircumcised, barbarian, Scythian, *slave and freeman*, but Christ is all, and in all" (3:11 emphasis mine). "Thataway, Paul, let my evil master have it!"

However, you can just feel the sigh of disappointment when those slaves then heard: "Slaves, in all things obey those who are your masters on earth" (3:22). Not only were these slaves disappointed, they were probably confused. "If all Christians are equal before God, then why should I have to obey my master? What if my master is not a Christian. Or better yet, what if he is?"

Paul explained that the reason we obey our employer is the same reason wives are to submit to their husbands and children are to obey their parents: God has placed all of us under someone's authority to teach us obedience and to accomplish His will in an orderly fashion. Without lines of authority, society will disintegrate. Paul added a word in verse 24 to encourage these Colossian slaves: "It is the Lord Christ whom you serve."

Some people hurry past that simple sentence without giving it much thought. But there are two powerful concepts about work in these few words. First of all, God is ultimately our employer and He is the One who will reward us one day. Regardless of whether you receive a Christmas bonus, a pay raise, or a promotion, God will some day compensate you for your good work: "Knowing that from the Lord you will receive the reward of the inheritance" (3:24).

The second concept I find here is that my job is one way of serving God. "The work of God" is not limited to evangelism and discipleship. Whether I am a plumber, a manager, or a schoolteacher, my job is an important way for me to serve the Lord.

Martin Luther said hundreds of years ago: "God even milks the cows through you!" Regardless of what our job is, we should realize that it is ultimately Jesus Christ for whom we are working.

2. We are to perform our work diligently. One of the first jobs I ever had was working at a Christian bookstore. The owner of the store was a wonderful Christian woman, but she had absolutely no ability or inclination to relax. After a big rush of customers, I wanted to take time, catch my breath, maybe down a soft drink. But she never would allow me to take a breath. "When there aren't customers, you need to straighten the shelves or dust the floor." (Now that I supervise a staff myself, I am more sympathetic with her attitude.) All of us employees would count the days until Thursday each week—that was her day off. And we would have a ball! One of us might sit in the back and read a book, while the other "covered" up front. We would enjoy a long lunch. We might even close up a little early if there wasn't much business.

However, our boss had a nasty habit of making an occasional surprise visit on her day off (something I also understand more). Whenever we would see her car pull up, we would signal to the other employees in the back room, and boy would we get busy! Until she left.

It is that kind of "work" Paul was discouraging when he said that we should obey "not with external service, as those who merely please men; but with sincerity of heart, fearing the Lord" (Col. 3:22). In other words, don't just work when the boss is looking. And don't sweep the dirt under the rug. Why? Because even if the boss doesn't see, your real Boss is always looking. He is the One you are really serving.

Instead, Paul said to perform your work—whatever your work is—"heartily." The word *heartily* could be translated "with all your heart" or "with all your energy."

In his excellent book *Secrets for Winning at Work*, Mike Murdock offers some practical tips for applying this principle of performing your work diligently:

Hear Your Boss's Instruction. Whenever your employer speaks, give her or him your undivided attention and total focus. I never will forget attending my first staff meeting as a new associate at First Baptist Church in Dallas. I was fresh out of college and full of enthusiasm. After the meeting, the staff dispersed, and Dr. Criswell, the pastor of the church, and I were left alone in the room. He walked with me up and down the U-shaped table that had been covered with a paper tablecloth for the meeting. "Robert, look at all of this doodling on the tablecloth. That is what most of these staff members do when I talk. They doodle! The reason I hired you is because you don't doodle. You're alert!!" Employers want to know they are being taken seriously when they speak.

Repeat Your Boss's Instruction. This will clarify that you and your employer are headed in the same direction. If you are unsure about something, ask her or him to explain.

Write Down Your Boss's Instructions. Make it a practice to keep pen and paper in hand whenever your employer gives you instructions. A long pencil makes up for short memory. By the way, knowing that you are writing down your employer's instructions will motivate him or her to be more accurate in his or her instructions.

Do What You Are Instructed to Do. Don't be like the slothful person described in Proverbs who always had an excuse for not doing his work. "The sluggard says, 'There is a lion in the road, a fierce lion roaming the streets!'" (Prov. 26:13). The truth is that lions would never roam the streets of a city. Yet, the lazy person is a master of rationalization.

Report Your Activity to Your Boss. The employees I value most are those who not only do what they are instructed, but who take time to report back to me their progress. That is going "the extra mile." And it also reveals an enthusiasm about their work.

Become Your Boss's Number One Problem-Solver. No employer likes an employee who is always "upwardly delegating" problems that he should be solving. As Murdock points out, "Your worth to your boss is determined by the problems you solve for him. You will only be remembered for two things: the problems you solve and the problems you create."[1]

3. *We are to perform our work honestly.* When Paul warned the slaves that "he who does wrong will receive the consequences of the wrong which he has done, and that without partiality," the Colossians knew exactly what situation Paul was addressing. In the Colossian church there was a Christian slave-owner named Philemon. One of Philemon's slaves, Onesimus, had stolen from Philemon and run away. When Onesimus arrived in Rome, he met the apostle Paul and became a Christian. Paul persuaded him that the right thing to do was to return to Philemon, even though it might mean death. Paul wrote the New Testament letter entitled "Philemon" to urge the Christian slave-owner to be merciful to Onesimus and allow him to make restitution for his theft.

Thus, when Paul wrote about a slave "who does wrong," he specifically is referring to theft. The most obvious application of this verse would be a prohibition against stealing money from our employer. Yet many Christians who would never think of dipping into the cash register regularly steal time or property from their employer.

Paul promised that whoever steals from his employer will suffer the consequences from his earthly employer, and will also be judged by his Heavenly Master as well.

A LESSON IN WORKER'S COMPENSATION

At this point in the reading of Paul's letter, I imagine the slave-owners were standing up, ready to vacate the church. "Boy, the pastor delivered another good one. I hope that no-account slave of mine was listening this morning!" "Wait just a moment," the pastor warns. "Paul is not through yet. He has a word for you, too." "'Masters, grant to our slaves justice and fairness, knowing that you too have a Master in heaven'" (Col. 4:1). What a revolutionary concept! Just as husbands have responsibilities in the home, Paul said that masters have obligations in the workplace. Let me paraphrase what Paul was saying to employers: "Yes, your employees need to perform their work diligently. Their work is ultimately for God. But remember that you work for someone, as well. You should treat your employees exactly like you want God to treat you."

Think about God's management style for a moment. How does He deal with His employees?

1. God spells out His expectations clearly. There is no confusion about what we are to do as Christians. God has given us a very detailed "personnel manual"—the Bible. He has clearly communicated what we are to do, what we are not to do, and the consequences of our actions.

Paul was saying that we should treat our employees in the same way. Nothing creates more friction between employers and employees than uncommunicated expectations. I think about one of my staff members whom I had judged as ineffective. In fact, his lack of performance made me angry because I kept thinking about the salary we were paying him. One Sunday evening after church, I sat down and wrote out all the things he was doing that I disliked, and all of the things he was not doing that I believed he should have been doing. This exercise was primarily for my benefit—it was a safe way to blow off steam.

But when I looked over the list, I asked myself if I had communicated all of these expectations to the staff member. I hadn't. The next day I called him in and shared with him a revised copy of my list. I detailed seven priorities for his specific job. I took the time to explain why these areas were such priorities to the church. He responded by saying, "I have been so overwhelmed by this job that I needed you to do this for me." Since that time, he has been performing magnificently. Clearly communicated expectations can reduce tension in the workplace.

2. God deals with us equitably. Paul encouraged employers to give their employees both "justice" and "fairness." The word *justice* carries the idea of giving employees what they deserve. Slaves received no salaries, but Paul encouraged their owners to adequately provide for their needs. He probably had in mind food, clothing, and medical care. When we provide for the needs of those under our supervision, we are reflecting the image of God who does not allow His children to go "begging [for] bread" (Ps. 37:25).

Employers, do you give your employees what they deserve? Does your company follow industry norms in:

➤ Direct compensation   ➤ Days off
➤ Retirement benefits   ➤ Breaks during the day
➤ Insurance   ➤ Child-care provisions
➤ Vacation time

Second, Paul encouraged us to treat employees with "fairness." This term refers to equality. If you are an employer, are you careful to be impartial in your treatment of employees? To favor one person over another on the basis of race, creed, personality, or another arbitrary factor violates the very character of God. In verse 25, Paul said that God judges us "without partiality."

3. God treats us compassionately. God sees us as more than tools of production, He has a deep concern for our lives. Paul encouraged us to have the same attitude toward our employees. We should demonstrate genuine concern for our employees' spouses, children, illnesses, and personal problems.

I learned that truth the hard way a number of years ago. When I first began my ministry, I mistakenly hired a secretary who was very deficient in her skills. She was moody, walked around the office in her bare feet, dressed inappropriately, and was constantly eating. I would even find food in her typewriter!

I couldn't take it any longer and had her transferred downstairs to the business office. I was so relieved. One morning she did not report to her new job. Finally, some people from the church went to her apartment to check on her. And they found her in a pool of blood. She had ended her life with a shotgun. Next to her body was a note describing the severe depression she had been experiencing—depression I had known nothing about. My interest in her had been strictly in her job performance. But her poor performance was symptomatic of a deeper problem.

Yes, we need to have standards at work. We should correct our employees when needed. Sometimes we must even dismiss them. Yet a heavenly-minded employer will mirror Christ's deep concern for those he supervises.

During World War I, Walt Disney and Ray Kroc (founder of McDonald's Corporation) were serving in the U.S. infantry. One day they found themselves in the same trench. During a lull in the battle, they both talked about their futures. They both admitted to dreaming that they would create great corporations with world-wide impact. They discussed what it would take for their new companies to succeed. This is what they determined:

1. Hire the best people you can find and pay them well.

2. Create a learning, creative, and expanding work environment.

3. Do all that you can to make them prosper personally.[2]

Paul suggested the same principles in Colossians 3. By treating our employees properly, we are not only ensuring our own success at work, but we are guaranteeing that one day we will be rewarded by our Master in heaven.

This section in Colossians reminds us that if we are truly becoming like Christ in our actions, attitudes, and affections, there will be some changes in our attitudes about work. Employees, being heavenly-minded means performing your work enthusiastically and diligently, because you are really working for God. Employers, being heavenly-minded for you means treating your employees the same way you want to be treated by God.

✳

ACTION STEPS

1. How does your job specifically help fulfill God's overall plan? _____

_____

_____

2. What are some practical things you could do to become more diligent in your work? _____

_____

_____

3. Think through recent assignments your employer has given you. Have you completed them? If not, make that a goal for the coming week.

4. Are you guilty of stealing money, property, time, or reputation from your employer? If so, ask for God's forgiveness and make restitution wherever possible.

5. If you are an employer or supervisor, think about the workers you supervise. Have you clearly communicated your expectations to them? Have you given them a written job description? Do you regularly give them constructive feedback about their performance? If not, make these items a priority for the coming year. You will enjoy both happier employees and a more productive business.

6. Are your employees being compensated fairly? Before the end of the year, make a study of your compensation benefits and compare them to industry norms.

7. Think about those with whom you most closely work. Do you know the names of your work associates' spouses and children? Are you aware of any emotional or spiritual struggles they are experiencing? Do you know if they are Christians? Pray for your associates daily and ask God to give you an opportunity to minister to them.

8. Memorize Colossians 3:22–4:1.

Epilogue

When I began this book many months ago, our church was in the beginning phase of raising four million dollars to renovate our church facilities. As I now finish this book and ship it off to the publisher, our church has also concluded its fund-raising effort. When we began the project, most of our members thought that the goal was impossible. But last Sunday morning we announced that our congregation had met and *exceeded* our goal. I have never witnessed such genuine excitement in a church!

However, I don't believe there was anyone in the audience last Sunday morning who believed this goal was accomplished through human effort alone. God gave us both the desire and the ability to accomplish this task for His glory. Although we expended a tremendous amount of effort during these last months, we felt His Spirit guiding and energizing us through the whole project.

As you finish this book you may think, "Whew! How can I ever do everything Paul has outlined in Colossians 3? Trying to permanently change my affections, attitudes, and actions is an impossible task!" It is, if you try to do it alone. But in Philippians 2:13, Paul reminds us of an important truth: "For it is God who is at work in you, both to will and to work for His good pleasure." The same God who has given you the desire to become like Christ has also given you the supernatural power—the Holy Spirit—to transform your life. In fact, He has already begun the project (see Phil. 1:6). But He wants your help.

So go ahead. Begin the renovation of your old actions, attitudes, and affections and start experiencing the good life *now*.

✳

Notes

Chapter One: All This . . . And Heaven, Too?

1. John MacArthur, *Your Completeness in Christ* (Chicago: Moody Press, 1984), 130.

2. Albert E. Brumley, "This World Is Not My Home" published in *Old Fashioned Revival Hour Songs* (Winona Lake, Ind.: The Rodeheaver, Hall-Mark Co., 1950), 4.

Chapter Two: Wanted: Dead *and* Alive!

1. Max Lucado, *In the Eye of the Storm* (Dallas: Word Publishing, 1991), 217.

2. R. Kent Hughes, *Colossians and Philemon* (Westchester, Ill.: Crossway Books, 1989), 89–90.

3. Charles R. Swindoll, *Living Above the Level of Mediocrity* (Waco, Tex.: Word Books, 1987), 147–49.

4. Charles R. Swindoll, *The Grace Awakening* (Dallas: Word Publishing, 1990), 114-15.

5. Kent Hughes tells the story in a slightly different way in the above-cited commentary on Colossians, 90.

Chapter Three: Just Say "No!"
1. Bobb Biehl, *Masterplan Your Life in One Day* (Laguna Niguel, Calif.: Masterplanning Group International, 1985), cover.
2. R. Kent Hughes, *Colossians and Philemon* (Westchester, Ill.: Crossway Books, 1989), 97.

Chapter Four: How to Dress for Success
1. Quoted in Warren W. Wiersbe, *Be Complete* (Wheaton, Ill.: Victor Books, 1981), 105.
2. Frank B. Minirth and Paul D. Meier, *Happiness Is a Choice* (Grand Rapids, Mich.: Butler Book House, 1978), 113.
3. Harold S. Kushner, *When Bad Things Happen to Good People* (New York: Avon Books), 117.
4. Charles R. Swindoll, *Three Steps Forward, Two Steps Back* (Nashville, Tenn.: Thomas Nelson Publishers, 1980), 149.

Chapter Five: Speech Therapy 101
1. In author's file. Source unknown.
2. Some ideas in this section came from Joseph Stowell's excellent book *Tongue in Check* (Wheaton, Ill.: Victor Books, 1983).
3. Quoted in Brian Harbour's *Brian's Lines* 7, no. 9 (September 1991).
4. Peggy Noonan, *What I Saw at the Revolution* (New York: Random House, 1990), 119.
5. James Patterson and Peter Kim, *The Day America Told the Truth* (New York: Prentice Hall Press, 1991), 45–46.
6. Calvin Miller in an article published in *Christianity Today*. Article in author's file. n.d.

Chapter Six: The Power of Positive Acting
1. R. Kent Hughes, *Colossians and Philemon* (Westchester, Ill.: Crossway Books, 1989), 102.
2. John MacArthur, *1 Corinthians* (Chicago: Moody Press, 1984), 338.
3. Article by Dan R. Barber in *The Dallas Morning News*.

Chapter Seven: The Secret to Lasting Peace
1. Quoted in Charles R. Swindoll, *Laugh Again* (Dallas: Word Publishing, 1991), 99.
2. Richard R. Melick, Jr., *The New American Commentary: Philippians, Colossians, Philemon* (Nashville, Tenn.: Broadman Press, 1991), 302.
3. A. L. Williams, *All You Can Do Is All You Can Do* (New York: Ballantine Books, 1988), 224.

4. Robert Jeffress, *Choose Your Attitudes, Change Your Life* (Wheaton, Ill.: Victor Books, 1992), 45.

5. Max Lucado, *The Applause of Heaven* (Dallas: Word Publishing, 1990), 77-78, 86-87.

6. Jeffress, *Choose Your Attitudes, Change Your Life*, 54.

7. Some of the ideas in this section appear in a slightly different form in my book *Choose Your Attitudes, Change Your Life*.

Chapter Eight: Bright Lights and Night Lights

1. Quoted in Ray Steadman, *Body Life* (Glendale, Calif.: Regal Books, 1972), 129–30.

Chapter Nine: Hooked on Others

1. Quoted by Ray Steadman in a sermon titled "Who Am I, Lord?" preached on March 13, 1977.

2. Gary Inrig, *The Parables* (Grand Rapids, Mich.: Discovery House Publishers, 1991), 119.

Chapter Ten: Count Blessings, Not Sheep

1. Vernon Grounds, *Radical Commitment* (Portland, Ore.: Multnoman Press, 1984), 122–23.

2. As told in a message "Grateful Hearts" published in *Brian's Lines*, vol. 6, no. 10.

3. Max Lucado, *In the Eye of the Storm* (Dallas: Word Publishing, 1991), 221, 225–26.

Chapter Eleven: Does Your Home Work?

1. Charles R. Swindoll, *Simple Faith* (Dallas: Word Publishing, 1991), xviii–xix.

2. From an article published in *The Dallas Morning News* and distributed by New York Times News Service titled "Women Pick Beach or Dinner over Sex in Poll," n.d.

3. James Dobson, *Hide or Seek* (Old Tappan, N.J.: Fleming H. Revell Company, 1979), 57.

4. Lloyd Cory, *Quotable Quotations* (Wheaton, Ill.: Victor Books, 1985), 132.

Chapter Twelve: Who's the Boss?

1. Mike Murdock, *Secrets for Winning at Work* (Tulsa, Okla.: Honor Books, 1993), 18–20.

2. Ibid., 141.

✳